OVERTHROWING
THE EVIL SPIRIT OF
SLEEPLESSNESS

A TRUE PERSONAL STORY

SWEDA WHYTE CRAWFORD

ISBN 979-8-89243-434-8 (paperback)
ISBN 979-8-89243-435-5 (digital)

Christian Faith Publishing
832 Park Avenue
Meadville, PA 16335
www.christianfaithpublishing.com

Printed in the United States of America

This book is dedicated to the Holy Spirit, the Helper of my Soul and the One who is behind all the revelation and knowledge shared in this book. All thanks, praise, glory, and honor be unto Him forever and ever. Amen.

Behold, I give unto you power to tread on serpents
and scorpions, and over all the power of the enemy:
and nothing shall by any means hurt you.

—Luke 10:19

CONTENTS

OVERTHROWING THE EVIL SPIRIT OF SLEEPLESSNESS is a very powerful spiritual warfare handbook that everyone should have.

It will bring a permanent solution to this enemy of *sleeplessness* if used according to the divine principles of the Scriptures, as there is absolutely no deliverance without the spirit of obedience to God's Word.

This book and its spiritual principles have helped me and many who have been bombarded with the demons or the evil spirits of restlessness, torment, panic, confusion, insomnia, sleeplessness, and the like, in the name of Jesus the Christ.

The Word of God is the sword of deliverance; it is the only warfare weapon that will defeat and destroy every form of evil spirit and demonic attacks that are programmed against your life.

It is a fact that there are millions of people in our world and also within our churches who are overpowered by the enemy of sleeplessness, and many have spent thousands, if not millions, of dollars, taking in harmful pills, medications, and different types of legal and illegal drugs just to enjoy or experience what should be a natural aspect of life, that is, good, healthy, peaceful, and deep healing sleep.

The law of Hosea 4:6 sums it up very well, as many of God's people are being destroyed because they lack spiritual knowledge on how to defeat and conquer this enemy that is living in many of our beds.

But let us not invite the spirit of discouragement in because the law of Proverbs 11:9b declares your deliverance, through the spirit of knowledge, and this is exactly what this book is all about. This book shares the author's personal experience and how she used the sword of God to destroy the enemy of sleeplessness and its accomplices, in the name of Jesus the Christ.

The Holy Spirit will then use this information to open your spiritual eyes and understanding into your deliverance if you seek to implement these simple but powerful spiritual principles taken from the Holy Bible, and put them into your daily practice, in the powerful name of Jesus the Christ.

ACKNOWLEDGMENTS

I would like to give thanks and acknowledgment to the God of my salvation. If it was not for the God of Moses who was on my side, surely, I would have been killed by Satan and his agents.

Secondly, I want to openly say a grateful thank-you to my husband, Mario, and our smart son, Daniel, for their love, support, and encouragement, especially during my challenging time of demonic attacks (sleeplessness). You are my heroes! Last but not least, a big thank you to all those who have positively impacted my life in any way. I am forever grateful, and God bless you.

Thank you guys, and I love you.

There are so many definitions for the word *sleep*. But sleep, according to the law of Isaiah 29:10, is a spirit. Sleep is a very important aspect of our lives. So in order for us to live healthy, functioning lives, we must sleep. Sleep restores, repairs, revitalizes and replenishes the body. And no human being or animal can go for a long duration without some amount of sleep. It is God who creates sleep and allows our bodies to relax and partake of it as outlined in the various scriptures here below.

> I will both lay me down in peace, and sleep: for thou, "Lord" only makest me dwell in safety. (Psalm 4:8)

> When thou liest down, thou shalt not be afraid: yea, thou shalt lie down, and thy sleep shall be sweet. (Proverbs 3:24)

Therefore, sleeping should be a natural and healthy aspect of a normal individual's life when it is in total balance for optimal health. One should not oversleep or under-sleep. When such activities occur or manifest in a person's life, it means there is an interference or an invasion in the natural realm of that person's spirit. In other words, there is an unwelcome intruder or an enemy that needs to get out immediately. Any prolonged visitation of this intruder could be very destructive and deadly. Hence, deliverance is of vital importance!

Please note that I am writing this book from a spiritual perspective, along with my personal encounter and deliverance from the spirit of sleeplessness, and not really from a medical perspective.

Because all things originated spiritually, including our sleep, as man is a spirit, housed in a physical body with the breath of God living in him.

> And the LORD God formed man of the dust
> of the ground, and breathed into his nostrils the
> breath of life; and man became a living soul.
> (Genesis 2:7)

Moreover, it is the designer and the maker of all lives who helps us to understand the importance of sleep to our physical bodies. No wonder Job declared that you "will lie down and sleep and none shall make you be afraid." It is indeed meaningless and vain not to enjoy good quality sleep as declared in the text below.

> It is vain for you to rise up early, to sit up
> late, to eat the bread of sorrows: for so he giveth
> his beloved sleep. (Psalm 127:2)

God made all living things to rest and respire, even the very plants, *especially* us, human beings.

If we look at the creation story, we see a clear blueprint of God's intention as it relates to us getting our rest and healthy peaceful sleep.

In addition, when we visit the law of Psalm 4, we are encouraged to lie down quietly and sleep when it is time to sleep as it is God our Creator who makes us sleep in safety.

As we explore this spiritual handbook together, we will discover how easy and simple it is for us to regain and maintain our peaceful healthy sleep lives, without the use of any harmful drugs, sleeping pills, medical procedures, gadgets, or money being used. Sleep is a gift that has been given to us by God our creator. We should not be deprived of it, and neither should we have to make the impossible attempts to pay monies to try and restore it.

CHAPTER 1

The Spirit of Ignorance Leads to Destruction

It was almost 1:00 a.m., the room was quiet, the bed was comfortable, and it was past my usual bedtime. I could hear the sound of the clock ticking, as my mind continued to wonder, *Why is it that I am not going off to sleep*? Even though I was extremely tired from my day's activities.

Oh, it is one of those nights, I thought, as once in a while, we all have nights when sleep just seems to run away from us. As I continued to ponder as to the reasons, I was not going off to sleep, I thought that maybe I was too anxious for the night's beauty rest, or, maybe it was because I was extremely tired; my body could not relax and go off to sleep. I continued to comfort myself with the spirit of ignorance, as he was my best friend, without me knowing it.

The long night of torture slowly went by without any form of sleep to my eyes, and it pushed me into a day of moodiness.

As I prepared to welcome a new night, I hurriedly completed my daily activities at an earlier time so that my body could have enough time to relax before going into its usual process of sleeping. So, I thought.

But lo and behold, this was another astonishing night and one to be remembered. The invisible enemy of sleeplessness appeared another night in my bed, and I could not understand why he was there.

My body was telling me it needed help. And like many of you, I started shopping for some of the most common sleeping remedies that are on the market. I shopped for teas, bath salt, and every other little relaxing "self-help" device or medication that I could find in the stores to use as a sleeping aid. I even shopped for books or anything that was related to sleep and sleeping. Yes, the spirit of ignorance had caused me to focus my attention in the wrong direction.

But let me not disappoint you because this vicious monster of sleeplessness continued, however, in a more aggressive manner.

This enemy was no doubt overpowering me as he forced me to make visitations to the walk-in clinics, doctor's office, acupuncture therapist, herbalist, and even to the office of the enemy himself, as I ignorantly sought help in the covens of these witches and the hypnotist or hypnotherapist's office.

This monster of sleeplessness was taking total control of my life; he was deteriorating my health and no doubt destroying my home and my family. I needed to stop him, but how? When the spirit of ignorance constantly had his cruel hands around my neck, choking me and telling me, "It is just a sleeping problem, and you will get over it in no time." As a matter of fact, he continued, "Everyone has these nights of sleeplessness. It is normal." And this was comforting, and I then thought I was not the only one with the monster of sleeplessness in my bed, and it would be okay. But can demons really speak the truth? Because it was not so. This vicious evil monster of sleeplessness continued to sink its evil tentacles into my sleep. I was forced for several years to visit various sleep clinics, herbalists, hypnotists, massage therapists, and doctors' offices with countless amounts of sleeping pills and other home remedies. The enemy of my sleep decided to push me deeper into depression and desperation of longing for what should have been a monophasic sleep pattern of a person's life.

When nothing seemed to have given me the help I needed, I later booked an appointment to see my doctor, Dr. V.

I was later scheduled by him to visit the sleep clinic. I was not excited as I knew it would have been another everlasting waiting list to see a sleep specialist.

The enemy of sleeplessness was a dangerous serpent in my bed, so I decided to wait for three months on an eternal waiting list. But what should I do in the meantime while waiting was my major concern. Waiting became another tormenting demon that I had to deal with. Could this be possible? How can I wait three months to see a sleep specialist? I questioned.

This was a setup, I concluded. But by whom is another question for which I needed answers.

I was desperately in need of sleep! I was desperately in need of some help! I needed anything that could help me to sleep because, at this time, I did not care what it was or how I came by it; I just needed sleep. My head was feeling extremely heavy. It felt as if I had a hundred pounds of weight just sitting consistently every day on top of my head. This feeling brought about a spirit of dizziness and made it more of a challenge for me to drive myself regularly. At times when driving, usually on one-way two-lane roads, I would often see four lanes, instead of two. Driving under such oppression was dangerous! So, I had to give up driving at times.

In the meantime, my doctor had prescribed some sleeping pills at a double dosage so they would be strong enough or stronger to aid sleep. I followed his advice, even when the pills made me feel sick and added to my dizziness at the time.

Nevertheless, I followed his advice and doubled the dosage. I started getting a little sleep with horrible dreams which added to confusing days. My appetite was also paying the price due to the adverse effects of the sleeping pills and medications. I felt very nauseated after my meals, and slowly my appetite began to fade away. I was losing weight rapidly; it was obvious that something negative was happening to me. I started to look and feel extremely sick. I became paler, and my skin went from firm to saggy, especially around my exhausted eyes and along my smile lines. I had looked twice my age as gray hair started to quickly outnumber the strands of my once thick black hair. This demon of sleeplessness began to celebrate with the other evil demonic spirits that were within my spirit. And, just like the woman with the spirit of infirmity, I needed to be loosed from the demon of sleeplessness, as outlined in the law of Luke 13:

> And when Jesus saw her, he called her to him, and said unto her, Woman, thou art loosed from thine infirmity. And he laid his hands on her: and immediately she was made straight, and glorified God. (Luke 13:12–13)

Poor concentration and lack of memory would at times put their evil hands around my neck, pulling me into a state of destruction. Inadvertently, I would always forget the simplest of things. There was no doubt that the evil spirit of forgetfulness was another spirit I had ignorantly invited in. I had lost touch with nature and the natural environment around me. I could not remember the peaceful sound of the soft and gentle breeze that once played with my bouncing thick black hair and gently caressed the smiling happy face I once had. Neither did my sense of feeling feel those heavy massaging raindrops that gladly massaged my naked toes that were always deliberate in creeping under the railings of my balcony and into the pounding rain.

All those natural desires were driven out by the evil and vicious demons that had occupied that place in my spirit. I was just left in a dark world to ponder and listen to the anxious sound of my tired heart.

All I could hear were the sounds of demons playing drums with my heart. Their evil oppression would escalate my heart rate and drive me into a panic. This form of manipulation was another doorway opener to the spirit of anxiety to enter my life.

But I was still ignorant of all that was happening to me at the time.

Every step of the way, another demon would introduce himself to my spirit, and ignorantly I would open the door of my spirit and let him in. I had totally lost count of the number of demonic spirits that were occupying my spirit.

Honestly, my days had looked like nights, and my nights were still darkness of sleeplessness, as I was battling with that major monster that was within my bed and head.

I was helping the monster of sleeplessness to prolong his stay in my life, as he continued to kill, steal, and destroy my life, due to my ignorance, as stated in the law of Hosea 4 below:

> My people are destroyed for lack of knowledge: because thou hast rejected knowledge, I will also reject thee, that thou shalt be no priest to me: seeing thou hast forgotten the law of thy God, I will also forget thy children. (Hosea 4:6)

A Spiritual Fight Using Physical Weapons

I will fast-forward to what happened during the coming weeks, months, and years.

Yes, I said it! The demon of sleeplessness stuck around for years; he became a permanent resident, and it seemed like leaving was not an option for him no matter how many physical weapons I had used on him. I must confess, he was winning the fights!

Therefore, please note that I had to go through years of restlessness, pain, hardship, confusion, and of course, sleeplessness to get my total deliverance and freedom, in the name of Jesus the Christ; so, I can honestly write what I am sharing with you now in this book.

I believe that God allowed me to come out alive and victorious to have compassion and mercy on those of you who are still battling with the demon of sleeplessness in your beds.

Now, doubling up on the dosages of the sleeping pills could only help me for a short time. Then the monster of sleeplessness returned mercilessly, and no amount of dosage of the pills could help as the battle was not physical but spiritual, now I know.

I discovered I was attacked by the spirit of witchcraft on the battlefield of life for years without knowing what it was. The spirit of sleeplessness was sent to my life to do one thing and one thing only:

to kill! It was sent or summoned from an evil altar "witchcraft altar." But first, it wanted me to suffer great afflictions and then terminate my life. But praise the Lord, the evil spirit of ignorance was drying up and the beautiful spirit of knowledge was growing like a tender plant in my life, paving the pathway into freedom and deliverance.

The spirit of ignorance was leaving slowly, not voluntarily, but I continued to destroy him, with the sword of the spirit; as the spirit of knowledge came slowly into my spirit.

I still can remember the moment like it was yesterday. For several nights, I would seek to go to bed to get at least an hour of sleep. I was desperate for even an hour of sleep, so I did not put my expectation very high of wanting more than an hour.

But even that was a very high expectation because I would doze off for twenty to thirty minutes, after which, some unseen being with cruel invisible hands would wake me up. It was like I was an actor in a horror movie.

How could this be? With absolutely no medical help, how could this problem be cured? I was driven from one healthcare practitioner to the next, from herbalist to acupuncturist, with countless amounts of medications and hundreds of dollars spent, hoping that someone or something would at least help me to get some sleep.

But it was a total waste of time, effort, and money. My health was quickly deteriorating, and my chance of survival was hanging in the balance.

I can remember on one occasion I telephoned a number I found on the Internet advertising a cure for insomnia. I booked my appointment and made sure I had the $120 for the forty-five-minutes service that this hypnosis guy (a wizard, now I know) would provide as discussed.

But upon arriving at his place, I got a strange feeling that something was not right about being there. However, because of my desperation, my husband accompanied me, and I went in. The hypnotherapist gave me a chair to sit in, and shortly after, he started talking. He was talking about his accomplishments. I was getting uneasy, and I was desperately wondering when treatment was going to start. I guess he sensed my agitations, and he quickly shifted his attention and engaged in asking me the questions I thought he was to ask. He asked me to describe to him what was happening to me.

He then told me to repeat the words *sleep, sleep, sleep, sleep*. I immediately concluded that he was a madman who also needed help.

I guess he was trying to put me into a trance. But it was not working; I quickly asked him to allow me to return to my truck for his payments. I hurriedly put my truck in the drive and drove away as I was already parked with the front of it facing the entrance. No, I did not pay him!

Another similar but different experience I have had was with a holistic herbalist, Dr. H., as I am not allowed to mention her real name without her consent. I also found Dr. H. through my desperate search on the Internet. I have often heard about herbalists and their treatments being successful, so my husband and I walked into her office with high expectations. As usual, there was a full lecture about their accomplishments and their track records of success. There was absolutely no doubt in my mind that she could help me with my sleeplessness. But after I experienced a strange occurrence of what she deemed as the administration of healing, I knew that something was not right, and again my spirit started feeling uneasy.

Dr. H. held out her right hand and took my right hand, then she told me to use my left hand to hold on to my husband's left hand, and then she used her other hand (left) to hold some instrument that magically lit up. "This is because of the energy in our hands," she stated.

She continued her magical experiments, and as she told me to stand, she placed her witchcraft hand on my tired forehead, she then held on to another set of instruments that had a light bulb without any form of electrical connection or current leading to it. The light bulb then also magically lit up, and she used this manipulation to explain energy. *Energy? What does energy have to do with me not sleeping?* I questioned myself.

As strange as it was, I was still waiting for her to tell me what exactly was happening to my sleep, but she later gave me a prescription with more than fifty different types of herbal pills. My first bill with all those medications was $750 at the time. I started taking these pills, and I discarded all those previous sleeping pills my doctor had given me.

I continued to take the herbal pills Dr. H. had given me for the next two weeks, but they too were useless.

Desperately, I returned to the office of Dr. H.

I told her that my condition was getting worse instead of better. She later changed my diet, and gave me another set of medication, in the form of cleansers. She explained that my body had toxins and needed cleansing before the products could work. *Foolish*, I thought, as she should have known better. Is she even a doctor? I questioned.

Surprisingly, my second bill was a bit less than the first one. However, I was only given three bottles of cleansers with another appointment to see her. I refused to be led into any more manipulation. I had planned to visit the acupuncturist someone had recommended. The person told me that he had a similar situation, and this was what had helped him.

Again, desperately I booked an appointment. My first treatment was an hour long. I was given some needles and a massage. Yes, it seemed like this was the solution to the problem because I had gotten at least some sleep the night after my treatment. The following night, the demons of restlessness came back, and I only managed to get about twenty minutes or so of sleep.

Eagerly, I went in for another treatment and explained my experience to the acupuncture therapist. She then told me that I needed some herbs with the treatment so that it can relax my body fully into sleep. Of course, anything to bring relief would be welcomed. So, I took the herbs.

However, to cut the story short, I continued to waste time and money in and out of her office until finally, I concluded that this was just another demon of deception and manipulation.

It is important to note that all this time, I have been a Christian for years, so I know that there is a God. But I prayed, it was not helping, and my situation had taken me all over the place in an attempt to find a physical solution for a spiritual problem.

I had called several pastors (so I assumed) to pray for or with me. But my situation continued to get only worse. On one particular desperate night, at about nine forty-five, my husband had to call the ambulance. The evil altars began to speak louder against my sleep and my life (now I know).

I had begun to urinate upon myself and my bed without feeling or knowing it. I was scared! I do not want to die, I confessed, but there was no help; an evil voice would answer me.

Desperately, my husband and I continued to cry out to God even though I, for one, did not know how. But I knew this was my last chance, just like blind Bartimaeus. And my faith had gripped the powerful hands of God. My life was about to change Just like this man's life in the story of the narrative below.

> And it came to pass, that as he was come nigh unto Jericho, a certain blind man sat by the way side begging: And hearing the multitude pass by, he asked what it meant. And they told him, that Jesus of Nazareth passeth by. And he cried, saying, Jesus, thou son of David, have mercy on me. And they which went before rebuked him, that he should hold his peace: but he cried so much the more, Thou son of David, have mercy on me. And Jesus stood, and commanded him to be brought unto him: and when he was come near, he asked him, Saying, What wilt thou that I shall do unto thee? And he said, Lord, that I may receive my sight. And Jesus said unto him, Receive thy sight: thy faith hath saved thee. And immediately he received his sight, and followed him, glorifying God: and all the people, when they saw it, gave praise unto God. (Luke 18:35–43)

God had directed us (my husband and I) to a simple but very powerful YouTube video on witchcraft. This video described the exact same thing I was going through at the time.

Minister Kevin L. A. Ewing at the time, now a pastor in Grand Bahamas, was telling us how he had overcome his witchcraft attacks and the evil altars that were speaking and operating against his life, health, finances, and destiny. And, hastily, we watched several more of his videos.

I quickly engaged in a three-day dry fast for the first time and followed the spiritual protocol of the law of Isaiah 58 according to the biblical narrative below.

> Cry aloud, spare not, lift up thy voice like a trumpet, and shew my people their transgression, and the house of Jacob their sins. Yet they seek me daily, and delight to know my ways, as a nation that did righteousness, and forsook not the ordinance of their God: they ask of me the ordinances of justice; they take delight in approaching to God. Wherefore have we fasted, say they, and thou seest not? wherefore have we afflicted our soul, and thou takest no knowledge? Behold, in the day of your fast ye find pleasure, and exact all your labours.
>
> Behold, ye fast for strife and debate, and to smite with the fist of wickedness: ye shall not fast as ye do this day, to make your voice to be heard on high. Is it such a fast that I have chosen? a day for a man to afflict his soul? is it to bow down his head as a bulrush, and to spread sackcloth and ashes under him? wilt thou call this a fast, and an acceptable day to the LORD? Is not this the fast that I have chosen? to loose the bands of wickedness, to undo the heavy burdens, and to let the oppressed go free, and that ye break every yoke? Is it not to deal thy bread to the hungry, and that thou bring the poor that are cast out to thy house? when thou seest the naked, that thou cover him; and that thou hide not thyself

from thine own flesh? Then shall thy light break forth as the morning, and thine health shall spring forth speedily: and thy righteousness shall go before thee; the glory of the LORD shall be thy reward. Then shalt thou call, and the LORD shall answer; thou shalt cry, and he shall say, Here I am. If thou take away from the midst of thee the yoke, the putting forth of the finger, and speaking vanity; And if thou draw out thy soul to the hungry, and satisfy the afflicted soul; then shall thy light rise in obscurity, and thy darkness be as the noon day: And the LORD shall guide thee continually, and satisfy thy soul in drought, and make fat thy bones: and thou shalt be like a watered garden, and like a spring of water, whose waters fail not. (Isaiah 58:1–12)

Immediately my sleep pattern improved the very first night of the fast. I could also feel the difference in my body, as the heavy weight I had on top of my head was totally lifted. By the end of my first three days of dry fasting and prayer, I was getting at least three hours of sound, deep, peaceful sleep each night without any form of sleeping medications or self-help relaxation products.

I praised the Lord for the miracle! I was excited!

God actually answered my prayers. But this was only the beginning of the journey to true lasting recovery and divine deliverance. I was determined to fight no matter what it took because I could hear the Holy Spirit telling me, "This is the only way out of bondage."

My husband joined me as we went on numerous fasting and prayer sessions. It was not an easy journey. I can still remember on two of those dry fasts I gave in; I quit the fast. I started feeling those great and dreadful hunger pains. I was new to this thing. But deep inside, I knew it was the only way out of bondage.

In addition to fasting and prayer, I would also feed the poor. This we consistently do even to this very day. The amazing miraculous results led me to develop a great love for fasting and prayer. Even to this day, I fast regularly. And no, the monster of sleeplessness is not in my bed anymore.

The results of these fasting and prayers brought me and my family closer to God. I became addicted to the Word of God that heals, delivers, and sets me free from the evil spirit of witchcraft. But it was not only fasting and prayer that brought me total deliverance because God will not heal our disobedience *as outlined in* Deuteronomy 28 below,

> But it shall come to pass, if thou wilt not hearken unto the voice of the LORD thy God, to observe to do all his commandments and his statutes which I command thee this day; that all these curses shall come upon thee, and overtake thee. (Deuteronomy 28:15)

I had to change the way I did Christianity. I had to walk in total obedience to the Word of God, and even though not perfect, the grace of God had kept and is still keeping me to do what is right according to the Scriptures. The law of Deuteronomy 28:1–2 had become my spiritual guide, as this is the only weapon to destroy the works of the devil in the name of Jesus.

> And it shall come to pass, if thou shalt hearken diligently unto the voice of the LORD thy God, to observe and to do all his commandments which I command thee this day, that the LORD thy God will set thee on high above all nations of the earth: And all these blessings shall come on thee, and overtake thee, if thou shalt hearken unto the voice of the LORD thy God. (Deuteronomy 28:1–2)

The law of God teaches that we must get spiritual knowledge and apply it for our deliverance. In addition, we must seek desperately to allow these spiritual laws to become applicable and practical in our daily lives to be overcomers as stated in Revelation 12:11.

> And they overcame him by the blood of the Lamb, and by the word of their testimony, and they loved not their lives unto the death. (Revelation 12:11)

My Deep Love for the Law of God

My encounter with evil altars and God's amazing deliverance gave me a deep love and desire for God's Word. I studied the Word for years—I still do—and with the help of the Holy Spirit, I take authority over demons and their works, in the name of Jesus, according to Luke 10.

> Behold, I give unto you power to tread on serpents and scorpions, and over all the power of the enemy: and nothing shall by any means hurt you. (Luke 10:19)

But the truth is, prior to my deliverance, I hated reading the Bible. Mostly because I did not understand it. I had absolutely no idea how important the law of forgiveness was and how much I needed to implement that particular law in my life.

So, as I learned the spiritual principles, I was ready to put them into action. I did not hesitate to do them, even though some of these spiritual laws were extremely challenging for me to activate in my life at the time. I needed spiritual maturity. But I was so willing and patient to do all that God wanted me to do.

Unforgiveness was one of my greatest challenges. But with the help of the Holy Spirit, I managed to defeat this evil giant.

I remember on several occasions I would try to find phone numbers or some form of contact information for persons whom I had hurt or who had hurt me (it didn't matter if they were the ones who had hurt me) to ask for forgiveness. I grew to love the law of Matthew 6 as it reminded me how much I am in need of God's forgiveness. God cannot forgive any of us until we choose to start forgiving one another as outlined in the text below.

> For if ye forgive men their trespasses, your heavenly Father will also forgive you: But if ye forgive not men their trespasses, neither will your Father forgive your trespasses. (Matthew 6:14–15)

I then realized how lighter my spirit had become with the powerful principles of God activated in it.

In studying the Scriptures carefully, the Holy Spirit opened my spiritual eyes, especially to the laws of Proverbs 28:27 and 19:17, and my heart welcomed the beautiful spirit of giving especially to the poor and needy. God loves the poor, and if we are in love with God, we too, will love what He loves.

> He that giveth unto the poor shall not lack: but he that hideth his eyes shall have many a curse. (Proverbs 28:27)

> He that hath pity upon the poor lendeth unto the Lord; and that which he hath given will he pay him again. (Proverbs 19:17)

As you continue to read through the chapters of this book, your spiritual knowledge will continue to increase, and if you plan to put in the work and walk in obedience to all of God's divine principles, you too will overthrow the evil spirit of sleeplessness, with the sword of God, in the name of Jesus the Christ. Developing a spirit of giving, especially to the poor, is also a powerful warfare weapon with which you can slay the giant of sleeplessness.

Finally, I had made a promise to God that if He would heal me and set me free, I would follow Him all the way and would give my life totally for His service. Yes, one way to maintain your deliverance is to always be ready to go wherever He sends you and tell of His excellent work in your life. You must be willing to teach all nations, tongues, and people the truth found only in the name of Jesus.

> Go ye therefore, and teach all nations, bap-
> tizing them in the name of the Father, and of the
> Son, and of the Holy Ghost: Teaching them to
> observe all things whatsoever I have commanded
> you: and, lo, I am with you always, even unto the
> end of the world. Amen. (Matthew 29:19–20)

God had delivered me from the powers of witchcraft!

It has been years, and the spirits of health, joy, peace, and happiness still to this day decorate my life. The power of God's Word is so real. I take absolutely no medications or vitamins, and I sleep like a baby, even if I am in a noisy environment. I did not return to any of those manipulating covens. I now fight the correct way using the powerful laws of God as my only weapon on life's battlefield. The God of Abraham delivered and set me free through the power of His Word, who is Jesus the Christ (see John 1:1).

In addition, He has given me a writing ministry wherein I share my life-changing journey and teachings on the invisible and visible worlds.

The war that we are in is derived from the invisible world, with our greatest enemies—demons, devils, and the entire kingdom of darkness—according to Ephesians 6:12.

> For we wrestle not against flesh and blood,
> but against principalities, against powers, against
> the rulers of the darkness of this world, against
> spiritual wickedness in high *places*. (Ephesians
> 6:12)

We need to stop the enemy before he stops us! Therefore, I would like to share this warfare handbook with you and your loved ones or anyone who wants to have a more intimate relationship with God. The enemy can be stopped. So please continue to read this book and gather all the spiritual tools to use in destroying this enemy of sleeplessness permanently out of your life, in Jesus' name.

Friends, I am a living testimony of God's healing power and deliverance from the evil spirit of witchcraft and sleeplessness. And if you or your loved ones are battling with this evil principality, you, too, will find the answer through studying and applying the powerful principles from the Holy Bible. It is a spiritual fact that power has shifted hands in my life and the Spirit of the Lord is upon me according to the powerful law of Isaiah 61.

> The Spirit of the Lord GOD is upon me; because the LORD hath anointed me to preach good tidings unto the meek; he hath sent me to bind up the broken hearted, to proclaim liberty to the captives, and the opening of the prison to them that are bound; To proclaim the acceptable year of the LORD, and the day of vengeance of our God; to comfort all that mourn; To appoint unto them that mourn in Zion, to give unto them beauty for ashes, the oil of joy for mourning, the garment of praise for the spirit of heaviness; that they might be called trees of righteousness, the planting of the LORD, that he might be glorified. And they shall build the old wastes, they shall raise up the former desolations, and they shall repair the waste cities, the desolations of many generations. And strangers shall stand and feed your flocks, and the sons of the alien shall be your plowmen and your vinedressers. But ye shall be named the Priests of the LORD: men shall call you the Ministers of our God: ye shall eat the riches

of the Gentiles, and in their glory shall ye boast yourselves. (Isaiah 61:1–6)

It is now your time to use the spirit of knowledge in identifying your real enemies according to 2 Corinthians 10 and wage war upon them in Jesus' mighty name. "For though we walk in the flesh, we do not war after the flesh." (2 Corinthians 10:3)

CHAPTER 2

Identifying the Enemy Using the Spirit of Knowledge

But through the power of knowledge and its application, you shall be delivered from the demon of sleeplessness, in the name of Jesus the Christ, according to Proverbs 11:9b.

There are many today, including Christians, who do not believe that there is an invisible world. Worst yet, they do not believe there are demons and devils walking up and down in our world and are responsible for all the evil and wickedness that are currently taking place in our physical world. These unclean creatures are our real enemies, and they must be stopped before they stop us. Many diseases are caused by the manipulative works of demonic spirits. We have seen many different stories in the Holy Bible of how demons distort the physical bodies of many persons; such examples can be seen as you continue to read through this chapter. But one very story that stuck within the corners of my mind is that of the woman who has been bent over for eighteen years. Maybe this particular story resonates with me because I am a woman who was also bound by a spirit of witchcraft and needed deliverance, and Jesus showed up!

Jesus the Christ opened our spiritual eyes to the fact that it was a spirit of infirmity that had this woman all bent over as He revealed the truth in the law of Luke 13 and showed us exactly what was really happening in the life of this woman, a daughter of Abraham.

> And he was teaching in one of the synagogues on the Sabbath. And, behold, there was a woman who had a spirit of infirmity eighteen years, and was bowed together, and could in no wise lift up herself. And when Jesus saw her, he called her to him, and said unto her, Woman, thou art loosed from thine infirmity. And he laid his hands on her: and immediately she was made straight, and glorified God. (Luke 13:10–13)

Like many of us, this woman was a child of God but was ignorant of what was causing her physical problem(s). Like myself in the past, she could not identify the enemy that was causing her discomfort due to a lack of spiritual knowledge. But praise God, Jesus saw this enemy and He bound and cast him out. The woman, like myself, was loose from the clutches of Satan, and from henceforth operated out of perfect peace and optimal health, according to Isaiah 26:3.

A second example of the works of demons can also be seen in the law of Luke 4 with the man who had an unclean spirit. It appears that everywhere the Word (Jesus the Christ; see John 1:1) shows up, deliverance takes place as unclean spirits become uneasy. Jesus has all the power and authority over demons and their works. And as He imparts deliverance through the spirit of knowledge, demons cry out and beg for mercy as the powerful warfare weapon of knowledge cuts their lies into pieces and destroys them out of the lives of once ignorant people. Such an example can be seen in the narrative below:

> Then He went down to Capernaum, a city of Galilee, and was teaching them on the Sabbaths. And they were astonished at His teaching, for His word was with authority. Now in the synagogue there was a man who had a spirit of an unclean demon. And he cried out with a

loud voice, saying, "Let us alone! What have we to do with You, Jesus of Nazareth? Did You come to destroy us? I know who You are—the Holy One of God!" But Jesus rebuked him, saying, ["Be quiet, and come out of him!" And when the demon had thrown him in their midst, it came out of him and did not hurt him. Then they were all amazed and spoke among themselves, saying, "What a word this is! For with authority and power, He commands the unclean spirits, and they come out." And the report about Him went out into every place in the surrounding region. (Luke 4:31–44)

With the spiritual understanding of God's word, we will need little or none of these medical practitioners around because more than 90 percent of sicknesses and diseases are the manipulative works of demons. However, the spirit of ignorance is one of the weapons that Satan uses to close many spiritual eyes, especially within the churches so that he can carry out his evil mandates. Spiritual knowledge is extremely important for our deliverance!

Satan uses the spirit of witchcraft to enter our dreams and plant evil seeds. No wonder the law of Matthew 13 exposes the works of darkness and seeks to educate us on the times that the enemy is most active in many ignorant lives. Satan uses our dreams to plant sicknesses, diseases, hardships, and the like in many of our lives. He does this at our most vulnerable times when we are unconscious, when we are sleeping, as stated in Matthew 13:25, "But while men slept, his enemy came and sowed tares among the wheat, and went his way."

There are many people who have ignorantly signed evil and deadly covenants with the enemy in their dreams. Likewise, many have eaten in their dreams; and as a result, they have been faced with numerous circular problems, including the premature spirits of death, poverty, sickness, failure, and the like. These deceptive and evil covenants can and should be broken. But if the spirit of knowledge is not present in our lives, how will we know what to do? The key out of bondage is spiritual *knowledge* and its application.

And even though this book is not about dreams and their interpretations, it is only wise for me to mention that all dreams must be given attention and must be interpreted by the Holy Spirit and the Scriptures. All demonic dreams, witchcraft dreams, and dreams from evil altars must immediately be cancelled using the blood of Jesus the Christ. However, according to the spiritual law found in Matthew 12, you must be on the side of righteousness before using the blood of Jesus to bind, cancel, rebuke, and cast out the enemy. Satan cannot cast out himself. In other words, you cannot be walking in disobedience to God's laws and then casting out Satan or destroying Satanic dreams in Jesus' name. If you do, what you are actually doing is setting up yourself for more demonic attacks as you would have been disobeying the spiritual law of Matthew 12:26, "And if Satan cast out Satan, he is divided against himself; how shall then his kingdom stand?"

Many people, especially Christians, are unaware that Satan has legal rights. Satan has legal rights to anyone who is walking contrary to the laws of God even if they are ignorantly walking in disobedience. Hence, we are told in 2 Timothy to study the Word to show ourselves approved unto God. So, there are absolutely no excuses for our disobedience!

No satanic roadblocks can stand in the way of a man who decides to equip himself with spiritual knowledge. Mountains of sicknesses and diseases will scatter with the powerful spirit of knowledge and its application.

Spiritual knowledge tells us that our warfare battles in the invisible are fought with the power of the Word. Yes, God's words on the tip of our tongues will send arrows of afflictions to the kingdom of darkness in the name of Jesus. No wonder the Bible has so much to say about the tongue because life and death still reside in it. We, therefore, should speak life to that which we want to live in our lives and death to that which we want to die out of our lives. The choices are really ours. But one thing is for sure, no one wants to live a life of suffering, plagued by a cruel spirit of sleeplessness.

God Gives the Believers Power Through the Spirit of Knowledge

If we notice how our God goes to work, He speaks! God speaks to the wind, the rain, the sun, the moon, the stars, and everything in His universe and they respond. On one occasion we witnessed the powerful commanding voice of Jesus speaking to the wind as He commanded it to be still as can be seen in Mark 4:39, "And he arose, and rebuked the wind, and said unto the sea, Peace, be still. And the wind ceased, and there was a great calm."

This, to me, proves that even nature knows and obeys the powerful voice of God. I know that many will argue that they are not Jesus, so it is not possible for them to rebuke the elements. And yes! You might be correct in some way because we are not Jesus. But be reminded that the spiritual law of John 14 still stands as it tells us the truth about who we are in Christ, "Verily, verily, I say unto you, He that believeth on me, the works that I do shall he do also; and greater works than these shall he do; because I go unto my Father" (John 14:12).

More so, we witness the obedience and faithful followers of God who use the power of God's Word to command the kingdom of darkness to take a bow. The apostle Peter shows us how the power of the Word works as he and John commanded the evil crippling spirit to leave the life of a beggar who had been crippled from birth.

Now Peter and John went up together into the temple at the hour of prayer, being the ninth hour. And a certain man lame from his mother's womb was carried, whom they laid daily at the gate of the temple which is called Beautiful, to ask alms of them that entered into the temple; Who seeing Peter and John about to go into the temple asked an alms. And Peter, fastening his eyes upon him with John, said, Look on us. And he gave heed unto them, expecting to receive something of them. Then Peter said, Silver and gold have I none; but such as I have give I thee: In the name

of Jesus Christ of Nazareth rise up and walk. And
he took him by the right hand, and lifted him up:
and immediately his feet and ankle bones received
strength. And he leaping up stood, and walked,
and entered with them into the temple, walking,
and leaping, and praising God. And all the people
saw him walking and praising God. (Acts 3:1–9)

This story proves to us that God has given us believers the power
to speak and command demons and devils to flee out of the lives of
people, including our own. Peter and John knew their authority in
Jesus, and they were not afraid to use it. "Behold, I give unto you
power to tread on serpents and scorpions, and over all the power of
the enemy: and nothing shall by any means hurt you" (Luke 10:19).

Jesus is reassuring us that our mouths are warfare weapons
against the evil powers that are waging spiritual war against us and
our lives.

Oh, if we New Testament believers of Jesus the Christ would
have used our mouths to speak the Word of God in commanding the
demonic winds of attacks to cease and leave our lives, the spirit of life
would put in His appearance as He raises back our Lazarus and fill
our lives with all the good things that God had in store for us from
the foundation of the world (see Ephesians 1:3).

On the other hand, while many Christians and the believers of
Jesus refuse to use the spirit of knowledge and the warfare weapon of
their mouths against the kingdom of darkness, the witches are not
afraid to indulge in their midnight enchantments to project their evil
against our lives. A witch will stay up night after night and chant just
to kill one person. Witches are full of patience as they work wickedly
to send in the spirits of sicknesses, poverty, and death if you lack spiritual knowledge as to how to fight back and defeat them.

And when it was day, certain of the Jews
banded together, and bound themselves under
a curse, saying that they would neither eat nor
drink till they had killed Paul. And they were

23

> more than forty which had made this conspiracy. And they came to the chief priests and elders, and said, We have bound ourselves under a great curse, that we will eat nothing until we have slain Paul. (Acts 23:12–14)

In addition, there are many, especially Christians, who still fail to recognize that there is some amount of truth in the common phrase that says "repetition deepens impression." It is also a fact that witches will chant the same evil words over and over their victim's name, photographs, handwriting, clothing, or any other personal items they can find of their victim(s). This they will do thousands of times while sitting or marching around their evil altars, just in an effort for evil to manifest in the life of such an individual.

And this is the very reason the Scriptures in Numbers 23 tell us that "there is no enchantment against Jacob, neither is there any divination against Israel." The twenty-one evil altars that Balaam the witch had set up could not take effect in the lives of the Israelites. Israel was walking in the commandments of God, and evil could not open the doors to come in unto them. The truth is, the Israelites at the time must have been using the powerful word of God on their tongues to slay their Goliaths. They had spiritual knowledge that guided them into walking in the way of the Lord. And as a result, the curses and the enchantments of the enemy could not have prospered in their lives.

> Surely there is no enchantment against Jacob, neither is there any divination against Israel: according to this time it shall be said of Jacob and of Israel, What hath God wrought! Behold, the people shall rise up as a great lion, and lift up himself as a young lion: he shall not lie down until he eat of the prey, and drink the blood of the slain. (Numbers 23:23–24)

The very same will happen to you if you seek to gain spiritual knowledge in knowing the will of God. We must, therefore, equip ourselves and use every opportunity wisely to study the word of God. In doing this, our faith in Him will grow and His Holy Spirit will help us to walk in total obedience to Him. However, if we keep on repeating negative evil words over our lives, our children, and others, we are no better than the witches who are sending curses from their evil altars to their victims. And God will hold us accountable for it, as we are in rebellion against the spiritual law of Ephesians 4 as stated here below.

> Let no corrupt communication proceed out
> of your mouth, but that which is good to the use
> of edifying, that it may minister grace unto the
> hearers. (Ephesians 4:29)

The thing I love about God is that He puts everything, concerning how we should govern our lives in His laws. This is so that we will not have any legal excuses on the day of God's final judgment.

> And I saw the dead, small and great, stand
> before God; and the books were opened: and
> another book was opened, which is the book of
> life: and the dead were judged out of those things
> which were written in the books, according to
> their works. (Revelation 20:12)

It is, therefore, our choice to do or not to do the law of God. But behold, whatever we are planting is exactly what we all will be harvesting as clearly outlined in the law of Galatians 6, "Be not deceived; God is not mocked: for whatsoever a man soweth, that shall he also reap" (Galatians 6:7).

When we can use the spirit of knowledge to identify the enemy and his works in our lives or the lives of others, we are well on our way to deliverance: and power has shifted hands from that of the enemy to ours. In addition, we will be better able to recognize the spiritual robbers of our destinies and wage war against them in the name of Jesus according to the law of Proverbs 6:31. As the chapter is brought to an end, let us ponder the Scriptures taken mainly from the book of Proverbs and see the importance of spiritual knowledge to our lives as we journey through a world that is loaded with evil and deep-rooted wickedness.

It is imperative for us to know that we should never at any point in time, take the Word of God for granted or ignore it. It is set in the universe for our protection, deliverance, blessings, and our eternal salvation in Jesus the Christ.

A Spiritual Look at Knowledge through the Eyes of the Proverbs

> The heart of the prudent getteth knowledge; and the ear of the wise seeketh knowledge. (Proverbs 18:15)

It is your responsibility to seek after knowledge.

> For the Lord giveth wisdom: out of his mouth cometh knowledge and understanding. (Proverbs 2:6)

The Word of the Lord is the only Word that gives true knowledge.

> The fear of the Lord is the beginning of knowledge: but fools despise wisdom and instruction. (Proverbs 1:7)

When we reverence God and His Word, we become spiritually smart and we are equipping ourselves with the warfare weapons that will defeat the enemies in the name of Jesus.

> When wisdom entereth into thine heart, and knowledge is pleasant unto thy soul; Discretion shall preserve thee, understanding shall keep thee. (Proverbs 2:10–11)

There is only one way to survive and it is by allowing the spirit of knowledge to enter into our hearts.

> Whoso loveth instruction loveth knowledge: but he that hateth reproof is brutish. (Proverbs 12:1)

It is clear that if we grow in love with God's principles, we will no doubt be equipped with the powerful warfare weapon of knowledge.

> For to one is given by the Spirit the word of wisdom; to another the word of knowledge by the same Spirit. (1 Corinthians 12:8)

Knowledge is a spiritual gift from God, and one will have to walk in His principles to activate this gift in his or her life. We must each study the Word of God in order to be approved by God.

> A wise man is strong; yea, a man of knowledge increaseth strength. (Proverbs 24:5)

Our spiritual strength, as well as our physical, will increase as we become more knowledgeable of God's words.

When I witness the lives of many within our churches, the demonic attacks and oppression that are overpowering many, the Holy Spirit led me to the same conclusion as that of Isaiah chapter 5. God's people are killed daily by evil altars, and only a few of us with spiritual lenses can see it.

> Therefore my people are gone into captivity, because they have no knowledge. (Isaiah 5:13)

Let us, therefore, seek after God because out of His mouth comes knowledge that will stop the enemy before he stops us!

CHAPTER 3

How to Stop the Enemy before He Stops You

There are many people who are still ignorant of the fact that Satan and his evil works can be stopped. As a matter of fact, Jesus has already destroyed the works of darkness. "He that committeth sin is of the devil; for the devil sinneth from the beginning. For this purpose the Son of God was manifested, that he might destroy the works of the devil" (1 John 3:8).

And God has given us, His faithful followers, the legal rights in the name of His Son, Jesus the Christ, to stop the enemy before he stops us (see Luke 10:19).

I also came to the realization that many people, like myself in the past, are suffering unnecessarily. They are suffering because they are lacking the truth about their victory in Jesus. The Scriptures declare that the Word of God is the only truth, while John 1:1 makes it abundantly clear that Jesus the Christ is the Word of God.

It is this Word, Jesus, that stops the enemy and restores our salvation in God through His painful death, burial, and triumphant resurrection from the grave.

> For I delivered unto you first of all that
> which I also received, how that Christ died for
> our sins according to the scriptures; And that

he was buried, and that he rose again the third
day according to the scriptures. (1 Corinthians
15:3–4)

Therefore, John 14 declares that no man can go to God except
through Jesus. "Jesus saith unto him, I am the way, the truth, and the
life: no man cometh unto the Father, but by me" (John 14:6).

The Word of God is, therefore, the only weapon and ammunition against Satan and his kingdom. The Word of God is the sword
that will and has destroyed principalities, powers, the rulers of the
darkness of this world, and all spiritual wickedness in high places,
including the spirits of sleeplessness and ignorance.

And having spoiled principalities and powers, he made a shew of them openly, triumphing
over them in it. (Colossians 2:15)

Let us look at the spiritual laws of John 1:14 and John 3:16
because these two laws will expose us to the fundamental understanding that we so much need to understand this chapter on how to
stop the enemy before he stops us.

And the Word was made flesh, and dwelt
among us, (and we beheld his glory, the glory as
of the only begotten of the Father) full of grace
and truth. (John 1:14)

As believers and faithful followers of Jesus, we are so grateful for
the law of John 1:14. Because this law in particular opens our spiritual eyes to the fact that Jesus the Christ came into our world and
was made flesh, just like you and me but without any form of sins.
Hence, He can relate to us fleshly human beings as He is touched by
the feeling of our infirmities. Jesus came to stop the enemy before
he stopped us by destroying the works of darkness on the cross of
victory. He came to give us the warfare weapon we need to defeat
the enemy in His name. The blood of Jesus the Christ stops the

enemy and gives us overcoming power to overthrow the evil spirit of sleeplessness.

However, in order to activate the power and authority over Satan and his agents, we must be actively engaging the law of John 14:15. We must love God and walk in obedience to all of His commandments. There is no way we can stop the enemy and his evil works in our lives if we are just like the enemy.

Likewise, the law of John 3:16 shows us that the love of God is also a powerful warfare weapon that is used to stop the enemy. God's love sent Jesus to die for us or in our place as declared in the Scripture.

> For God so loved the world, that he gave his only begotten Son, that whosoever believeth in him should not perish, but have everlasting life. (John 3:16)

The love of God in your life will, therefore, be a powerful warfare weapon that will allow you to overthrow the evil spirit of sleeplessness and stop the enemy before he stops you. The nature of the enemy, Satan is always to kill, steal, and destroy lives and destinies. He is a hater, and those who do not have the love of God in their lives are a reflection of the enemy and his nature (see John 8:44).

When we practice loving one another, we gain victory over Satan and his evil works in our lives. We thereby stop him before he stops us.

Satan knows the spiritual rules, and he uses them to manipulate and defeat the ignorant, rebellious, and disobedient. It is totally impossible to defeat or stop Satan if the love of God is not active in our lives. First John 4:8 (NKJV) says, "He who does not love does not know God, for God is love."

Becoming Victorious over Satan

Our victory over Satan and his kingdom depends on two things. It depends on our knowledge and most importantly, our choices.

> And if it seem evil unto you to serve the LORD, choose you this day whom ye will serve; whether the gods which your fathers served that *were* on the other side of the flood, or the gods of the Amorites, in whose land ye dwell: but as for me and my house, we will serve the LORD. (Joshua 24:15)

As creatures or children of God, we are given the freedom of choice. God expects us to choose whom we will serve: He, God our creator and the giver of all lives, or he, Satan the enemy and the destroyer of all lives.

> The thief cometh not, but for to steal, and to kill, and to destroy: I am come that they might have life, and that they might have it more abundantly. I am the good shepherd: the good shepherd giveth his life for the sheep. But he that is an hireling, and not the shepherd, whose own the sheep are not, seeth the wolf coming, and leaveth the sheep, and fleeth: and the wolf catcheth them, and scattereth the sheep. (John 10:12)

Our choices will determine our victory on the battlefield. To win this war (the war of sleeplessness), we must be covered under the winning blood of Jesus the Christ.

> And they overcame him by the blood of the Lamb, and by the word of their testimony; and they loved not their lives unto the death. (Revelation 12:11)

Before we do our selection (or make our choices), let us therefore ponder intensively upon the law of Deuteronomy 30:15–16 as this is a direct warning from the God of all flesh.

> See, I have set before thee this day life and good, and death and evil; In that I command thee this day to love the LORD thy God, to walk in his ways, and to keep his commandments and his statutes and his judgments, that thou mayest live and multiply: and the LORD thy God shall bless thee in the land whither thou goest to possess it. (Deuteronomy 30:15–16)

However, in order for us to truly activate our power of choice in choosing wisely and in choosing good over evil and life over death, we must equip ourselves with the spirit of knowledge. Spiritual knowledge of the Word of God will open our spiritual eyes to the truth and the way—who is Jesus the Christ.

God is the lover of our souls. It is His job to deliver, restore, protect, and keep us in safety if we hearken unto the voice of His commandment, according to Proverbs 1:33: "But whoso hearkeneth unto me shall dwell safely, and shall be quiet from fear of evil."

It is therefore imperative for us to understand that victory over the enemy will only be possible in our lives if we faithfully seek to do exactly what James 1:22 commands. We must hear (study) the Word of God and then do as the Word tells us. When we do, we are no doubt becoming like the Word (see John 1:1).

It is sad, even though it is the truth that many today, especially church folks, still believe that their emotional activities of crying, shouting, and sowing of seeds (monies) along with unruly speaking in tongues will give them victory over Satan (see John 5:4).

But the truth is, engaging in these activities and going against the spiritual laws of the Bible is rather a curse that invites more demons and their evil activities to operate in their lives. Jeremiah 17:5 says, "Thus saith the LORD; Cursed be the man that trusteth in man, and maketh flesh his arm, and whose heart departeth from the LORD."

Many people refuse to accept the fact that God is also governed by His laws, and we must follow His divine principles as outlined in the Holy Bible to have the victory that is given to us through Jesus and His shed blood. Again, the Scriptures are clear, by knowledge, the just (you) shall be delivered (see Proverbs 11:9b).

God's kingdom is governed by principles, rules, and laws. The very same for Satan's kingdom, even though both kingdoms are totally opposite. God is the creator of all things with all the power, and Satan is the evil creature, the enemy, the imitator with a limited amount of power. The kingdom of darkness needs the kingdom of light to exist as all power belongs to God (see Isaiah 45 and Psalms 62).

> I form the light, and create darkness: I make peace, and create evil: I the LORD do all these things. (Isaiah 45:7)

> God hath spoken once; twice have I heard this; that power belongeth unto God. (Psalm 62:11)

However, God respects all His divine rules, and Satan has rights within these rules, but he too must respect all of God's laws. I did not say that Satan obeys these laws or is expected to obey God's laws because we all know that is impossible; Satan is the master of disobedience, but he must respect all of God's divine laws.

Yes, Satan will have the rights to anyone who is walking in disobedience to God's divine laws until that person renounces Satan and his works, repents, and asks God to forgive him, in the name of Jesus the Christ.

When this spiritual process happens and is maintained with total obedience and love to do God's laws, then this person now has the legal rights, through Jesus the Christ to activate power and authority over the works of darkness.

> And when He had called unto Him His twelve disciples, He gave them power against

unclean spirits to cast them out, and to heal all manner of sickness and all manner of disease. (Matthew 10:1)

Jesus the Christ has made it absolutely clear in the law of Luke 10:19 that we the believers have the authority through Him, and His power, to destroy demons, devils, and their works out of our lives, including the demon of sleeplessness.

Catch this! Demons have absolutely *no* legal right to occupy a believer's life.

God's Law Is for Our Good

God's law is His principles, rules, ordinances, precepts, and commandments that He uses to govern His universe. The law of God is perfect as it converts the soul of man unto righteousness. However, the law in itself cannot save us because it is our faith in God that saves us. The law is like a mirror as it shows us what is right from what is wrong in God's sight. Romans 3:20 (NIV) says, "Therefore no one will be declared righteous in God's sight by the works of the law; rather, through the law we become conscious of our sin."

The Scriptures are clear; it is not they who hear the law are just in God's sight, but they who hear and do the law of God are justified in His sight. It is in the book of James chapter 1 that we understand that we must not only be hearers of the law but also doers of it. "But be ye doers of the word, and not hearers only, deceiving your own selves" (James 1:22).

The law is for our good; it opens our spiritual eyes and points us to the absolute truth, who is Jesus the Christ. It is through the law of God that we understand our requirements and our duty, both to God and man. God's law is just and perfect according to Psalm 19:7.

When we obey the law of God, Satan cannot put his evil hands on us. One of the many reasons my sleep was attacked by the spirit of witchcraft was my disobedience to the law of God. If I was obedient in studying the law as stated in 2 Timothy 2:15, my spiritual eyes would have been opened. And instead of suffering unnecessarily, I would have fought the correct way and overthrew or stopped the evil spirit of sleeplessness. To be disobedient and ignorant of the law of God will cause us to suffer as we activate the spirit of death in our lives. Satan will try and prevent us from knowing or studying the Bible because he knows that if we are knowledgeable about God's law, the evil works of his kingdom cannot come close to us as the curses cannot come into our lives until there is a cause, according to Proverbs 26.

> As the bird by wandering, as the swallow
> by flying, so the curse causeless shall not come.
> (Proverbs 26:2)

It is not until we transgress the law of God that Satan and his evil works will gain entrance into our lives and our sleep.

> Whosoever committeth sin transgresseth
> also the law: for sin is the transgression of the law.
> And ye know that he was manifested to take away
> our sins; and in him is no sin. Whosoever abideth
> in him sinneth not: whosoever sinneth hath not
> seen him, neither known him. (1 John 3:4–6).

No wonder Isaiah 5:13 tells us the truth about our sufferings.

> Therefore my people are gone into captiv-
> ity, because they have no knowledge: and their
> honourable men are famished, and their multi-
> tude dried up with thirst.

God wants us to lead healthy, happy lives. He wants us to enjoy our families and our friends; He wants us to enjoy His beautiful cre-ation and to walk in obedience to Him, as this is the only way to our eternal happiness in Him.

We can't enjoy these things and have a Godly attitude if we don't get sleep. Satan knows this!

35

God cannot be like the enemy, Satan! Therefore, we must walk in the spirit of obedience to divine order to truly please Him.

Whether we believe or not, whether we like or accept it or not, man—you and I—were created for God's glory and must give to God all that He requires from us in order to have what He says is ours in the name of Jesus. God is a reciprocal God, we cannot receive the power, abundance of blessings, healing, deliverance or victory until we give to Him what He asked us for.

But how will we know what God requires of us if the spirit of ignorance is living within our spirits? It is in the book of Micah 6 that God explains His answer to this question. Because God's desire is for all of us to walk in righteousness.

> Will the LORD be pleased with thousands of
> rams, or with ten thousands of rivers of oil? shall
> I give my firstborn for my transgression, the fruit
> of my body for the sin of my soul?
> He hath shewed thee, O man, what is good;
> and what doth the LORD require of thee, but to
> do justly, and to love mercy, and to walk humbly
> with thy God. (Micah 6:7–8)

God expects us to study His words so that we will know the strategies of the enemy and also to know our victorious rights as children of God. It is only in studying and doing exactly what God commands that we can totally be free from the enemy, including the enemy of sleeplessness.

When we study the Word of God for ourselves, we are becoming obedient to the commandments of God, and we are gaining the approval of God in our lives, as stated in 2 Timothy 2.

> Study to shew thyself approved unto God, a
> workman that needeth not to be ashamed, rightly
> dividing the word of truth. (2 Timothy 2:15)

It is only in studying the Word that we can understand that God expects us to prosper and be in good health, even as our souls become prosperous in Him. As children of God, we should enjoy beautiful, peaceful sleep when it is time for us to sleep. Sleep is a gift from God to us, and we should not have to be deprived of something so important and crucial for our optimal health and our survival. However, when we are ignorant of spiritual laws, we quickly accept the lies from the enemy. We take whatever he gives us and try to do the best we can with it. We seek after sleeping pills, medications, sleeping clinics, hypnotists or hypnotherapists, massage therapists, and other sleeping aids—hoping to find a man-made solution for a spiritual problem (see Jeremiah 17:5).

The spirit of ignorance totally hides the fact that it is God the Creator who had designed and created sleep and gave it unto us as free gift. Therefore, if something goes wrong with our sleep, He, God, should be the one to fix it. After all, He knows how to. Satan is a liar, a deceiver, and a murderer; and he is currently destroying many homes, families, and lives with the evil spirit of sleeplessness even as you are reading this book (see John 8:44; Isaiah 14:12–14; and Ezekiel 28:14–16).

Satan does this by pushing many away from the truth and from the God who is more than able to restore our sleep and, by extension, our health (see 3 John 2). "good health"

Catch this! Satan is the one who created the problem of sleeplessness in the first place, even though we are responsible for our choices (see Joshua 24:15). And then he sends us to seek help in various places in an attempt to totally destroy us. If we study God's Word and make it applicable to our lives, we will find out that Satan is not that smart because how can he create the problem and then try to offer a solution? But again, this is Satan. He is a manipulator. He comes to kill, steal, and destroy lives and destinies, and he does this through his evil spirits and his agents, including the system of witchcraft (see 1 Kings 13:4 and 1 Kings 21:9–13).

Friends, if we refuse to study the Word or the law of God for ourselves and be delivered, Satan, his demons, and his agents will continue to stone our sleep and, by extension, our lives with stones of affliction and eventually death, if not delivered, by the blood of Jesus the Christ.

> Beloved, I wish above all things that thou mayest prosper and be in health, even as thy soul prospereth. (3 John 3)

It is only in studying the Word of God that we will realize how important each of us is to God. Our sleep matters. God wants us to have a healthy and balanced life, and sleeplessness is not a part of His plans for you, as declared in the law of Psalm 127,

> It is vain for you to rise up early, to sit up late, to eat the bread of sorrows: [for] so he giveth his beloved sleep. (Psalm 127:2)

Friends, when we know that the God of the universe does not sleep, we can quietly go off to sleep. God's protective and loving eyes are keeping us safe, even while we lay down to sleep.

> Behold, he that keepeth Israel shall neither slumber nor sleep. The LORD is thy keeper: the LORD is thy shade upon thy right hand. The sun shall not smite thee by day, nor the moon by night. The LORD shall preserve thee from all evil: he shall preserve thy soul. (Psalm 121:4–7)

Both Proverbs 3:24 and Psalm 4:8 are also God's laws. God expects us to lie down and go to sleep when it is time for sleep, knowing that greater is He inside of our spirits than the demon of restlessness or sleeplessness.

> Ye are of God, little children, and have overcome them: because greater is he that is in you, than he that is in the world. (1 John 4:4)

God knows that we have an enemy, and this enemy is going about like a roaring lion, seeking anyone who will give attention to him. Therefore, we need to study the Word of the Lord and walk in obedience to His divine law so that we can become vigilant and sober, especially in a world like ours.

> Be sober, be vigilant; because your adversary
> the devil, as a roaring lion, walketh about, seek-
> ing whom he may devour. (1 Peter 5:8)

It is extremely important that the minds be protected so that we can fight the enemy of our souls without getting hurt. It is the powerful Word of God that protects our minds. It is therefore a wise spiritual practice to ensure that we put on the helmet of salvation and have the sword of the spirit in our hands.

> And take the helmet of salvation, and the
> sword of the Spirit, which is the word of God.
> (Ephesians 6:17)

Remember, we cannot go to war without understanding the war that we are fighting. And this war that we are all a part of, even if we choose not to fight, is a spiritual war that requires spiritual weapons to fight our invisible enemies, including the evil spirit of sleeplessness.

God's laws: God expects us to:
Prov. 3:24 "when you lie down, you will not be afraid; when you lie down, your sleep will be sweet."
Psalm 4:8 "I will lie down and sleep in peace, for you alone, O Lord, make me dwell in safety."

CHAPTER 4

Understanding the War
You Are Fighting

It is the Lord Himself who tells us that we are all in a wrestling battle.
But this wrestling is not against other human beings like ourselves. It
is an invisible fight with evil invisible beings, and it, therefore, calls
for invisible weapons to war in this fight.

Many of us are going about each day beaten up by our opponents, the devil and his agents because we are still not aware that we
are on a spiritual battlefield and we must fight. Spiritual ignorance of
the law of God is Satan's greatest weapon of mass destruction against
humanity. One of the amazing things about God is that He tells us
exactly what will happen to us if we refuse to do as He commands.
He also shows us a vivid picture by listing all the possible evil that we
are up against as stated in Ephesians 6 below.

> For we wrestle not against flesh and blood,
> but against principalities, against powers, against
> the rulers of the darkness of this world, against
> spiritual wickedness in high *places*. (Ephesians
> 6:12)

But our God is faithful. He will never leave us unprotected,
nor will He leave us empty-handed and stranded for the enemy to

destroy us. Hence, in the law of 2 Corinthians 10, He makes it crystal clear that the weapons that we each should use against the enemy should be spiritual as it is spiritual warfare. These spiritual weapons against the enemy and his kingdom are mighty through God, and they are specifically designed by God for the pulling down of demonic strongholds in our minds. As I was writing this aspect of the chapter, the Holy Spirit began to show me a deeper understanding of 2 Corinthians 10:4–5 because now my spiritual eyes and ears began to open as the Holy Spirit showed me that all of Satan's efforts and aims are to destroy our minds. He does this by clouding our minds with demonic imaginations, self-exaltation, and evil thoughts. But God wants us to use His words to pull down every demonic stronghold out of our minds as stated by the apostle Paul in 2 Corinthians 10. Hence, meditation of the word should be practiced.

> For the weapons of our warfare are not carnal, but mighty through God to the pulling down of strong holds; Casting down imaginations, and every high thing that exalteth itself against the knowledge of God, and bringing into captivity every thought to the obedience of Christ. (2 Corinthians 10:4–5)

Let us go more in-depth as we continue to examine our warfare weapons according to the law of Ephesians 6.

> Wherefore take unto you the whole armour of God, that ye may be able to withstand in the evil day, and having done all, to stand. Stand therefore, having your loins girt about with truth, and having on the breastplate of righteousness; And your feet shod with the preparation of the gospel of peace; Above all, taking the shield of faith, wherewith ye shall be able to quench all the fiery darts of the wicked. And take the helmet of salvation, and the sword of the Spirit, which is

the word of God: Praying always with all prayer
and supplication in the Spirit, and watching
thereunto with all perseverance and supplication
for all saints. (Ephesians 6:13–18)

We need to understand that the armor of God, though divided
into different spiritual protective pieces of coverings, functions as
one. The armor of God is really Jesus the Christ, who is the truth;
God's righteousness; the gospel of peace; salvation; the Word of God;
and the faith in God. Notice that Paul encourages us to take the
whole armor because in Christ there is no division. Jesus the Christ
and His shed blood is our weapon of warfare. We cannot go to battle
unless the marks of the Lord Jesus are upon us, as stated by Paul in
Galatians 6:17.

From henceforth let no man trouble me: for
I bear in my body the marks of the Lord Jesus.
(Galatians 6:17)

It is a spiritual fact that we must dress for battle! I like the fact
that we already know our opponents and where they are located. We
also know the most powerful ammunition that they always use on the
battlefield. But to target our warfare arrows directly at the targeted
enemy, we must be able to identify him. Satan knows that it is with
the minds that we serve the Lord, so if he can get the mind of a man,
he can rob him of the opportunity and the joy to serve the Lord.
Therefore, God is reminding us of how to handle these demonic
activities that are set up against our minds by using the powerful
sword of God to arrest them and bring them under subjection to
the will of God. We must take authority over every evil work of the
enemy. At no point in time should our thoughts be left unguarded
by the power of the Holy Spirit. We should not allow our minds and
our thoughts to go where God forbids us. We must take on the mind
of Christ in order to be victorious as stated in Philippians 2:5, "Let
this mind be in you, which was also in Christ Jesus."

I want to move in deeper as we take somewhat of a close-up look at the characteristics of our major opponents on the battlefield. Because, for far too long, mankind has been ignorant of the characteristics of our real invisible evil enemies known as *principalities, powers, rulers of darkness of this world, and spiritual wickedness in high places* of whom Satan is the head or the leader.

It is in the law of Matthew 12:43–45 that God exposes the major characteristics of an unclean spirit. We are told that these evil spirits have similar characteristics to us human beings. Even though they are disembodied invisible beings, they can talk, walk, and reason. They have a will, and they can display emotions; they are very intelligent with self-awareness. And they are also referred to as *the angels which kept not their first estate*, according to Jude 1:6.

> When the unclean spirit is gone out of a man, he walketh through dry places, seeking rest, and findeth none. Then he saith, I will return into my house from whence I came out; and when he is come, he findeth it empty, swept, and garnished. Then goeth he, and taketh with himself seven other spirits more wicked than himself, and they enter in and dwell there: and the last state of that man is worse than the first. (Matthew 12:43–45)

The number one goal of unclean spirits is to inhabit physical bodies, especially human beings, in order to carry out effectively their evil works. Therefore, we are warned in the law of 1 Peter 5:8 to be sober and vigilant, especially in a world where people are desperate for popularity, fame, and all that glitters. In 1 John 4:1, we are seriously commanded not to believe every spirit but try the spirits whether they are of God because many false prophets are gone out into the world. The God of the universe sees and knows all things before they happen, and He gives us spiritual knowledge beforehand so that we can be set free from the wiles of the devil.

These enemies are evil creatures that are invisible to our physical eyes and only can be seen if God allows us. However, the occult world and people who practice sorceries, voodoo, witchcraft, fortune-telling, enchantment, and divination, including tarot cards, palm, and teacup readings along with crystal-gazing are able to demonically interact with these evil beings for evil purposes (see Deuteronomy 18:9–12). In Acts 16, we witness a high-ranking demonic power at work as it possesses the life of a young girl who was used to profit her owners. But Paul, who had the power and the anointing of the Holy Spirit on his life, recognized that it was a familiar or a monitoring spirit that had possessed her; and he rebuked the evil spirit, and it went out from her. The very same evil, demonic activities are taking place today even among many church people.

> And it came to pass, as we went to prayer, a certain damsel possessed with a spirit of divination met us, which brought her masters much gain by soothsaying: The same followed Paul and us, and cried, saying, These men are the servants of the most high God, which shew unto us the way of salvation. And this did she many days. But Paul, being grieved, turned and said to the spirit, I command thee in the name of Jesus Christ to come out of her. And he came out the same hour. (Acts 16:16–18)

In addition, Simon Magus the sorcerer was no different as he too had a familiar spirit, and had for many years, bewitched the people of Samaria that he was under the anointing of God's Holy Spirit. He was looked upon as some highly respected man in Samaria, and all the people feared him. But he was a wizard who had long bewitched the people in that town with his witchcraft.

> But there was a certain man, called Simon, which beforetime in the same city used sorcery, and bewitched the people of Samaria, giving out

> that himself was some great one: To whom they
> all gave heed, from the least to the greatest, say-
> ing, This man is the great power of God. And to
> him they had regard, because that of long time he
> had bewitched them with sorceries. (Acts 8:9–11)

Witchcraft has long been around, and many seek after this evil power to kill, steal, and destroy the lives and destinies of the ignorant and the disobedient. It is in the book of 1 Samuel 28 that we witness Saul seeking the service from the witch of Endor to know about the outcome of his future because God had turned His back on Him and refused to answer him. Saul sought after a woman with a familiar spirit to render him help in bringing up Samuel from the grave. However, this was not the spirit of Samuel, as Samuel was a righteous man of God. But the Scripture says that Saul perceived it was Samuel (see also 1 Samuel 28:14b).

> Then said Saul unto his servants, Seek me
> a woman that hath a familiar spirit, that I may
> go to her, and enquire of her. And his servants
> said to him, Behold, there is a woman that hath a
> familiar spirit at Endor. And Saul disguised him-
> self, and put on other raiment, and he went, and
> two men with him, and they came to the woman
> by night: and he said, I pray thee, divine unto
> me by the familiar spirit, and bring me him up,
> whom I shall name unto thee. (1 Samuel 28:7–8)

Nonetheless, all these practices are abominations unto God, and they who practice or seek after such services are also committing abominable acts, according to Revelation 21:8.

When a witchcraft spirit is sent against a person, it is sent to kill, steal, and destroy the person's life and destiny.

However, all evil spirits need an altar from which to operate, including the spirit of witchcraft. The truth is that the evil altars are demonic platforms where evil spirits meet with evil human spirit(s) to carry out evil mandates against the lives of their victim(s). Yes, an evil altar is also known as the evil spiritual base where demonic sacrifices are made to Satan in exchange for his evil mandate to occur in the lives of those who have been summoned at the evil altar. When I searched the Scriptures to find a suitable example of evil works that are done at evil altars, the Holy Spirit opened my eyes to Balaam and his wizardry as can be seen in the powerful narrative below.

> And Balaam said unto Balak, Build me here seven altars, and prepare me here seven oxen and seven rams. And Balak did as Balaam had spoken; and Balak and Balaam offered on every altar a bullock and a ram. And Balaam said unto Balak, Stand by thy burnt offering, and I will go: peradventure the LORD will come to meet me: and whatsoever he sheweth me I will tell thee. And he went to an high place. And God met Balaam: and he said unto him, I have prepared seven altars, and I have offered upon every altar a bullock and a ram. And the LORD put a word in Balaam's mouth, and said, Return unto Balak, and thus thou shalt speak. And he returned unto him, and, lo, he stood by his burnt sacrifice, he, and all the princes of Moab. And he took up his parable, and said, Balak the king of Moab hath brought me from Aram, out of the mountains of the east, saying, Come, curse me Jacob, and come, defy Israel. How shall I curse, whom God hath not cursed? or how shall I defy, whom the LORD hath not defied? For from the top of the rocks I see him, and from the hills I behold him: lo, the people shall dwell alone, and shall not be reckoned among the nations. Who can count the dust of Jacob, and the number of the fourth part of Israel? Let me die the death of the righteous, and let my last end be like his! And Balak said

unto Balaam, What hast thou done unto me? I took thee to curse mine enemies, and, behold, thou hast blessed them altogether.

And he answered and said, Must I not take heed to speak that which the LORD hath put in my mouth? And Balak said unto him, Come, I pray thee, with me unto another place, from whence thou mayest see them: thou shalt see but the utmost part of them, and shalt not see them all: and curse me them from thence. And he brought him into the field of Zophim, to the top of Pisgah, and built seven altars, and offered a bullock and a ram on every altar. And he said unto Balak, Stand here by thy burnt offering, while I meet the LORD yonder. And the LORD met Balaam, and put a word in his mouth, and said, Go again unto Balak, and say thus. And when he came to him, behold, he stood by his burnt offering, and the princes of Moab with him. And Balak said unto him, What hath the LORD spoken? And he took up his parable, and said, Rise up, Balak, and hear; hearken unto me, thou son of Zippor: God is not a man, that he should lie; neither the son of man, that he should repent: hath he said, and shall he not do it? or hath he spoken, and shall he not make it good? Behold, I have received commandment to bless: and he hath blessed; and I cannot reverse it. He hath not beheld iniquity in Jacob, neither hath he seen perverseness in Israel: the LORD his God is with him, and the shout of a king is among them. God brought them out of Egypt; he hath as it were the strength of an unicorn. Surely there is no enchantment against Jacob, neither is there any divination against Israel: according to this time it shall be said of Jacob and of Israel, What hath God wrought!

Behold, the people shall rise up as a great lion, and lift up himself as a young lion: he shall not lie down until he eat of the prey, and drink the blood of the slain. And Balak said unto Balaam, Neither curse them at all, nor bless them at all. But Balaam answered and said unto Balak, Told not I thee, saying, All that the LORD speaketh, that I must do? And Balak said unto Balaam, Come, I pray thee, I will bring thee unto another place; peradventure it will please God that thou mayest curse me them from thence. And Balak brought Balaam unto the top of Peor, that looketh toward Jeshimo And Balaam said unto Balak, Build me here seven altars, and prepare me here seven bullocks and seven rams. And Balak did as Balaam had said, and offered a bullock and a ram on every altar. (Numbers 23:1–30)

It is crystal clear from the story above that neither Satan, demons, nor mankind can go beyond what God permits. The enemy knows that God is the one who has all the powers, and if God says the curses of witchcraft shall not stand against your life and destiny, that is exactly what He means; and that is exactly how it will be. Whenever God speaks, it formulates spiritual laws that echo throughout all of His universe, both in the visible and the invisible. And His voice stands forever (see Matthew 24:35).

And when Balaam saw that it pleased the LORD to bless Israel, he went not, as at other times, to seek for enchantments, but he set his face toward the wilderness. (Numbers 24:1)

Therefore, Numbers 24:13 serves as a reminder to all the evil spiritual "Balaams" and their evil altars that will seek to rise up against your sleep. Whom God blesses, let no man curse; and your sleep is blessed by God and cannot be cursed by the devil, in Jesus' name.

> If Balak would give me his house full of silver and gold, I cannot go beyond the commandment of the LORD, to do either good or bad of mine own mind; but what the LORD saith, that will I speak? (Numbers 24:13)

Satan will imitate all that God does if God permits him. However, Satan cannot go beyond the laws of the Lord and curse those whom God already blessed.

In 1 Kings 13:1–6, we also witnessed an evil altar being serviced by another one of Satan's servants. Jeroboam was in his coven servicing his evil altar when a young prophet of the Lord showed up with a warning. Jeroboam refused to take heed to the voice of the Lord and shortly after found himself with a withered hand. Catch this! God always gives a warning before destruction.

> And, behold, there came a man of God out of Judah by the word of the LORD unto Bethel: and Jeroboam stood by the altar to burn incense. And he cried against the altar in the word of the LORD, and said, O altar, altar, thus saith the LORD; Behold, a child shall be born unto the house of David, Josiah by name; and upon thee shall he offer the priests of the high places that burn incense upon thee, and men's bones shall be burnt upon thee.
>
> And he gave a sign the same day, saying, This is the sign which the LORD hath spoken; Behold, the altar shall be rent, and the ashes that are upon it shall be poured out. And it came to pass, when king Jeroboam heard the saying of the man of God, which had cried against the altar in Bethel, that he put forth his hand from the altar,

saying, Lay hold on him. And his hand, which he put forth against him, dried up, so that he could not pull it in again to him. The altar also was rent, and the ashes poured out from the altar, according to the sign which the man of God had given by the word of the LORD. And the king answered and said unto the man of God, Intreat now the face of the LORD thy God, and pray for me, that my hand may be restored me again. And the man of God besought the LORD, and the king's hand was restored him again, and became as it was before. (1 Kings 13:1–6)

The hands of the wicked witches will wither and dry up if they still insist on erecting evil altars against the lives of the righteous who know how to engage in spiritual guerilla warfare of fasting and prayer.

Crying Out to God

Evil altars against your life should be scattered using the powerful blood of Jesus the Christ.

If there are doorways of sinful practices, unconfessed sins, or ignorance in a person's life, evil spirits will gain entrance to that life and wreak havoc, as any form of sin is a spiritual legal ground on which the evil altars will speak against such life or lives.

Because of my personal experience of being attacked by the spirit of witchcraft, which had caused me to experience extremely painful years of sleeplessness, I can easily identify the spiritual signs and the physical manifestations of this evil being and its attack on sleep.

When a person's sleep is under demonic or witchcraft attacks or evil altars, sleeplessness will occur suddenly, without absolutely any warnings.

Another thing about evil altars working against a person's sleep is the pattern and the time that this restless spirit will put in his appearance. Many witchcraft attacks are programmed for the night. The powers of the nights are dangerous if you do not know how to plead the blood of Jesus the Christ against them. They will deal with you if you refuse to deal with them.

Some witchcraft attacks are seasonally programmed and even though the signs and occurrences are similar in their evil works, no two people will experience the exact same pattern of attacks so it is imperative for each of us to understand the war we are fighting.

The spiritual attack on my sleep lasted for several years on and off. It was somewhat similar to the story of the bewitched boy in Matthew 17:15.

This boy often had attacks but not all the time. It was only when the evil altar was serviced that the witchcraft spirit was sent to do their evil against his life. The operation and curses of witchcraft are dangerous, especially for those who are spiritually ignorant of its operation. However, the law of Matthew 17 shows us exactly what our first approach should look like while on this spiritual battlefield. We should cry out for God's mercy, pending we have repented of our sins.

> Lord, have mercy on my son: for he is luna-
> tic, and sore vexed: for ofttimes he falleth into
> the fire, and oft into the water. (Matthew 17:15)

However, our crying out should be more than a physical one. It should be done out of repentant hearts while reminding God of His words and His promises according to the law of Isaiah 43:26. We should search the Scriptures prayerfully and command the law of protection to work for us through the voice of faith in the name of Jesus the Christ. I love the warfare law of Isaiah 7:7 as this powerful spiritual reminder helps us to understand that the weapons of evil altars, bewitchment, and enchantment of the witches shall not stand. It is our responsibility to fight wickedness with the Word of the Lord by first repenting of our sins and next by faithfully reminding God of

His Word. Then we stand still and see the salvation of our God upon the lives of the enemies (see Esther 7:10).

Catch this! A person who does not know God's Word cannot remind God of His Word. As this reminder is also a spiritual process. It means to activate faith while believing the Word, who is Jesus the Christ (see John 1:1).

Our lives must be pleasing to God before power can shift hands from the enemies to ours.

Now that I have looked back at my experience of suffering and pain as a victim of witchcraft, I now understand exactly the reason(s) many, especially church folks, cannot identify these evil spirits and their evil works in their lives. I also understand why many within the churches are dying prematurely as a result of the evil works of witchcraft that are set against their lives. The spirit of witchcraft is a thief; he is a destroyer, and also a killer. He will not leave any life that cannot identify him and cast him out using the blood of Jesus.

> Then said the king to the servants, Bind him hand and foot, and take him away, and cast him into outer darkness, there shall be weeping and gnashing of teeth. (Matthew 22:12)

Many within our churches are not able to identify the spirit of witchcraft because they do not believe he is real or he exists. It is a fact that many Christians' belief systems stop at the same distance as their peripheral views. They do not believe in the unseen world, but ironically, they claim to believe in Jesus the Christ who is also in the invisible or the unseen world. There are very few churches and their members who believe that witchcraft is real and that Christians can be oppressed and attacked by evil spirits. I must confess that I was once a part of such religious group or church. And my conclusion now is, God's people are perishing while the weapons to destroy the enemy are at their fingertips.

I can still remember, that no matter how much human effort I had put into securing a peaceful night of sleep, it was useless as my battles were not physical. So, no amount of relaxation, medication, or anything physical could have given me a peaceful deep and healthy sleep. The altar(s) would not have allowed it, now I know, as the evil sacrifices were continuous at these altars. It is a fact that the devil needed a human agent with whom he could have carried out his evil mandates.

> your adversary the devil, as a roaring lion,
> walketh about, seeking whom he may devour. (1
> Peter 5:8)

And in my case, some hateful and evil human beings were ready to partner with the devil to destroy me. As a matter of fact, these evil people went to the devil with my name and identification, in an attempt to first steal my happiness, destroy my family, and then finally kill me. They did not wait for Satan to seek their help; they went to him seeking his help.

They had it all in their evil demonic diaries with the dates and the time their evil mandates would materialize and come to fruition in my life. They wanted me out of the land of the living, but they wanted to make sure I suffered long and hard, as death without long and slow suffering was not enough payment to feed their evil spirits of jealousy. But I am grateful for my haters who partnered with Satan in an attempt to kill me because if they had not done their evil against my life, how else would I have written this book with all these experiences that will prayerfully make its way around the globe and set the captives free, in the victorious name of Jesus the Christ. Better yet, how else would I have developed a spiritual addiction to the laws of God, which bring deliverance to the captives? I can tell you that your enemies are your greatest assets; they serve a purpose, so bless them and pray for them according to the law of Luke 6. Their wickedness against you will catapult you into divine success if you are seeking to deal with these attacks with the powerful Word of God. I always encourage people to love their human enemies, bless them, and forgive as we overcome all evil done to us with the spirit of good (see Romans 12:11–21).

> But I say unto you which hear, Love your enemies, do good to them which hate you, Bless them that curse you, and pray for them which despitefully use you. But love ye your enemies, and do good, and lend, hoping for nothing again; and your reward shall be great, and ye shall be the children of the Highest: for he is kind unto the unthankful and to the evil. (Luke 6:28, 29, 35)

CHAPTER 5

Overthrowing the Evil Spirit of Sleeplessness

From my personal experience and encounter with witchcraft and its attacks, I cannot stress the point enough that, knowledge, and obedience to the laws of God are the *only* weapons against any form of evil, especially the evil spirit of witchcraft.

Here is the truth: If we love God as we claim, then why is it that the spirit of witchcraft has its upper hand in many of our lives? God tells us in the gospel of John that if we love Him, we should become obedient to His commandments: "If you love me keep my commandments" (John 14:15).

If we are obedient to the commands of God, it is rather *impossible* for Satan to put his evil hands on our lives; this includes the spirit of witchcraft and all other forms of wicked spirits in high places.

I am writing to you as if I have met you before because your deliverance can be today, right now, as you are reading this book, without paying any form of money or engaging in any form of rituals. You don't need a pastor, bishop, priest, or pope to secure your deliverance. You do not need to even go to a church building. You can receive your deliverance in the comfort of your home or wherever you are. God is omnipresent! All you will need is a changed mind—a mind that loves Jesus and wants to please Him. The message of deliverance is really simple but very effective and powerful because it is the amazing and powerful sword of God.

Overthrowing the enemy of sleeplessness is really simple as it depends on two things:

1) Your spiritual knowledge and understanding of God's Word
2) Your love and obedience to the laws of God

There is absolutely no doubt that if you love God, you will do exactly what He commands.

But what are the commandments? God's commandments are all that He asks us to do and also that which He tells us not to do. With a deep understanding of how God operates through His divine law, we are well on our way to overthrow the enemy of our sleep. Just as sleep is a spirit, the enemy is a spirit and God is a spirit. It is clear that we are fighting in the spirit with spiritual unclean beings. There is absolutely nothing physical about this fight. Hence, you will need all the spiritual tools possible to pull down the demonic strongholds that are summoned against your sleep. Please revisit chapter 4 of the book.

Again, we should search the Bible for all the promises that God outlined for our health and sleep. But first, we need to find Scriptures that glorify and praise God for who He is. We need to remind God of His tender mercies to us His children and confess consistently the law of Psalm 84:11:

> For the Lord God is a sun and shield: the
> Lord will give grace and glory: no good thing will
> he withhold from them that walk uprightly.

Next, search the Scriptures and write out or highlight all the spiritual laws that show how God has subdued the enemy. In the book of Joshua 6, we witness the powerful hands of God working through the life of an obedient Joshua to subdue the enemies by tearing down the evil witchcraft wall altars of Jericho. Jericho was destroyed and all its inhabitants, except for Rehab the harlot and her household.

> Now Jericho was straitly shut up because of the children of Israel: none went out, and none came in. And the Lord said unto Joshua, See, I have given into thine hand Jericho, and the king thereof, and the mighty men of valour. (Joshua 6:1–2)

All it took was obedience and faith in the voice of God on the battlefield to overthrow the enemies of Jericho. It is no different with you and the enemy of sleeplessness. You must activate the warfare weapons of faith and obedience in God and His Word.

I cannot help it as my mind quickly commemorates the story of Esther 3:5–15. However, in verses 9–10, we witness another powerful destruction of the enemy, as the enemy, Haman, died on the very evil altar he had set up for the faithful Mordecai. Your enemies will die in your stead if you seek to fight God's ordained way.

> And Harbonah, one of the chamberlains, said before the king, Behold also, the gallows fifty cubits high, which Haman had made for Mordecai, who spoken good for the king, standeth in the house of Haman. Then the king said, Hang him thereon. So they hanged Haman on the gallows that he had prepared for Mordecai. Then was the king's wrath pacified. Esther 7:9–10

The Bible is clear—God is not partial; He is the same God who overthrew these wicked and deadly enemies at Jericho, and He is the same one who will overthrow the enemy of your sleep if you follow the same divine principles as Joshua, Esther, and all the other individuals, patriarchs, prophets, and disciples of old.

Another powerful way to overthrow the enemy is to be consistent in following the truth as stated in the law of John 14.

>Jesus saith unto him, I am the way, the truth,
>and the life: no man cometh unto the Father, but
>by me. (John 14:6)

It is only in knowing and applying the truth, which is Jesus Himself, that we can truly be set free from the hands of the enemies. The enemies, namely, Satan, principalities, powers, and rulers of this dark world as stated in chapter 4 of this book.

Let us stop giving the devil of sleeplessness legal rights. He is a defeated foe! Whenever each of us decides to walk in the truth and the light, submitting ourselves unto God, we will have victory in all departments of our lives including victory over the evil power of sleeplessness. Knowing and walking in the truth means total submission unto God as stated in the spiritual law of James 4.

>Submit yourselves therefore to God. Resist
>the devil, and he will flee from you. (James 4:7)

But maybe you are like me who, in the past, asked the question, "How do I walk in the truth?" Here is the simplest answer to your question: we walk in the truth by becoming obedient to divine authority. And what does that mean? Well, obedience to divine authority means you are living a God-approved life. You are doing exactly as He commands in the Holy Bible.

Another powerful weapon that should be used in overthrowing the enemy of sleeplessness is the righteousness of the Lord Jesus the Christ. The Bible tells us in 2 Corinthians 5:21 that *God made him, Jesus to be sin for us, who knew no sin; that we might be made the righteousness of God in him.* This is powerful because, when we are God's righteousness, we have the mind of Jesus, and no demon nor devil can defeat us. It is the righteousness of the Lord that turns the house of the wicked into ruin (see Proverbs 21:12b).

When we take on the righteousness of the Lord Jesus Christ by walking in obedience to divine authority, we become like Jesus, and the kingdom of the enemy will be afraid of us. Deuteronomy 28:10 says, "And all people of the earth shall see that thou art called by the name of the Lord; and they shall be afraid of thee."

It is God's righteousness that will slay the plans of the enemies against your divine destiny. It is like a sword, and it will also cut the evil spirits of witchcraft, sleeplessness, evil altars, and their works out of the hands of the wicked that are spiritually working against you, according to the law of Micah 5:12: "And I will cut off witchcrafts out of thine hand, and thou shalt have no more soothsayers."

Many people refuse to believe or to understand that another powerful way of fighting the enemy is to share the gospel of Jesus the Christ. As God's righteousness in Christ, we must hearken to the voice of God's commandment as stated in the law of Matthew 28:19: "Go ye therefore, and teach all nations, baptizing them in the name of the Father, and of the Son, and of the Holy Ghost."

When your feet are shod with the preparation of the Gospel of Jesus, the demon of sleeplessness cannot come upon you. Demons and the devils are afraid of the Word (see John 1:1).

If you will start to share the Gospel of Jesus the Christ with others, the power of the Word will be so sharp on the tip of your tongue that demons and devils will scatter and flee according to Deuteronomy 28:7: "The LORD shall cause thine enemies that rise up against thee to be smitten before thy face: they shall come out against thee one way, and flee before thee seven ways."

If your feet are shod with the preparation of the Gospel of Jesus the Christ, just like the Syrians, God will cause your enemies to hear a sound and flee when no man pursues them, according to 2 Kings 7:

> For the Lord had made the host of the Syrians to hear a noise of chariots, and a noise of horses, even the noise of a great host: and they said one to another, Lo, the king of Israel hath hired against us the kings of the Hittites, and

the kings of the Egyptians, to come upon us. (2
Kings 7:7)

It is the Word of God that brings salvation to all. It is the Word
that sets us free from the captivity of Satan. So, speaking and sharing
the Gospel of Jesus the Christ will continue to bring deliverance to
your life, in Jesus' name.

The spirit of sleeplessness, which is from Satan's kingdom, cannot survive within a righteous spirit. As the righteous spirit attracts
and invites the power of God.

The truth is, we are unable to fulfill our God-given duties,
including overcoming the evil spirit of sleeplessness if the beautiful
spirit of faith is not embedded within our spirits. The Bible is clear:
without faith, we cannot please God, and all our lives must be pleasing to God in order for us to be His righteousness or have our feet
shod with the Gospel of peace.

We are encouraged to take the shield of faith so that we can
spiritually block, stop, defeat, and destroy the lies of the enemy. Yes,
the lies of the enemy are like fiery darts that are constantly fired at us
daily. No wonder the songwriter John H. Yates pend the song "Faith
is the victory that overcomes the world."

Anyone who ever gets what God promises will have to walk on
the pathway of faith. The spirit of faith will destroy the evil spirits of
doubt, fear, anxiety, and depression. It will shield and protect us from
every form of evil coming from the kingdom of darkness, in Jesus'
name. When we think about Abraham, it was by faith that he had to
offer up that which he loves when he was tested by God. It is a fact
that no man can ever follow God without the spirit of faith in Him.

And it came to pass after these things, that
God did tempt Abraham, and said unto him,
Abraham: and he said, Behold, here I am. And
he said, take now thy son, thine only son Isaac,
whom thou lovest, and get thee into the land of
Moriah; and offer him there for a burnt offering

upon one of the mountains which I will tell thee
of. (Genesis 22:1–2)

In overthrowing the enemy of sleeplessness, we must also put
on the helmet of salvation found in the powerful blood of Jesus the
Christ. But what is salvation according to the Scriptures? The law of
Isaiah 12:2 answers such a question. "Behold, God is my salvation; I
will trust, and not be afraid: for the Lord, Jehovah is my strength and
my song; he also is become my salvation."

Salvation is from the Latin word that means "to be saved."
Therefore, we cannot go up against the kingdom of darkness unless
we are saved by God's grace through Jesus the Christ and His shed
blood. Salvation is for everyone as it is the free gift of freedom from
our sins that Jesus made possible by taking the punishment for our
sins on the cross.

> For mine eyes have seen thy salvation, which
> thou hast prepared before the face of all people; A
> light to lighten the Gentiles, and the glory of thy
> people Israel. (Luke 2:30–32)

But God allows us the power of choice to choose if we want to
be saved.

> And if it seem evil unto you to serve the
> Lord, choose you this day whom ye will serve;
> whether the gods which your fathers served that
> were on the other side of the flood, or the gods
> of the Amorites, in whose land ye dwell: but as
> for me and my house, we will serve the Lord.
> (Joshua 24:15)

Salvation is for the unrighteous according to Mark 2:17: "When
Jesus heard it, he saith unto them, they that are whole have no need
of the physician, but they that are sick: I came not to call the righteous, but sinners to repentance." And when we accept this free gift

from God, we have the legal spiritual right to trample upon all spiritual serpents and scorpions of our sleep, in the name of Jesus, and nothing shall harm us (see Luke 10:19).

In Ephesians 6:17, Paul also reminds us that salvation is also a helmet that should be worn on our heads for spiritual protection. But I like the fact that he also tells us that the sword of the Spirit, which is the Word of God, must also go along with the helmet of salvation. Because when we are saved, the Word of God protects our minds from evil thoughts and strongholds coming from Satan's kingdom. It is, therefore, important that we keep on our helmet of salvation as any form of doubt that we allow to enter our minds is a doorway for evil spirits to gain entrance to our spirits. The spirit of doubt in our minds will destroy us and stop the powerful hands of God from working on our behalf.

It is with the minds that we serve the Lord, and once the mind is contaminated with the spirit of doubt, we cannot truly serve God until we repent and seal our minds with the blood of Jesus. Please note that it is impossible to win any spiritual battle without the helmet of salvation and the sword of the Spirit, which is the powerful Word of God that gives us the peace that passes all understanding.

When the beautiful spirit of peace lives inside your spirit, you will be blessed according to the law of Matthew 5. And absolutely, no curse of sleeplessness can come unto you.

The righteous are the peacemakers of the earth, so they are blessed and absolutely no curse of infirmities and sleeplessness should overpower them, in the name of Jesus (see also Numbers 23:8).

Blessed are the peacemakers: for they shall
be called the children of God. (Matthew 5:9)

The evil spirit of sleeplessness will not and cannot survive in anyone who is walking and resting in the peace of God.

What exactly is peace? So many people think that peace is the physical comfort that one enjoys. Peace is a spirit from God's kingdom. The Spirit of peace is activated in our spirits when we are constantly studying and meditating upon the Word of God. It is impossible for an unrighteous person to possess the beautiful spirit of peace as the love for God's law must first decorate the garden of his life.

> Great peace have they which love thy law:
> and nothing shall offend them. (Psalm 119:165)

> Thou wilt keep him in perfect peace, whose
> mind is stayed on thee: because he trusteth in
> thee. (Proverbs 26:3)

When we have the peace of God in our lives, absolutely nothing can harm us or offend us. The spirit of peace will not come into our lives because we want him to come, but he will only come if we love God and His Word.

Again, our minds, therefore, should be wrapped up in the powerful words of God as we seek to engage in constant meditation of the Word. Personally speaking, I love to read the Word; but at times, it is not always possible to have a Bible in our hands 24-7 to read. So, I would often recommend that you get an audio copy of the bible and play it while you do your daily activities or better yet, while you go off to bed.

Let us remember that it—is the Prince of Peace who had overthrown the kingdom of Satan, including the enemy, the spirit of sleeplessness (see Isaiah 9:6).

The Bible reminds us that we should pray without ceasing. This means that we should consistently be talking to God as prayer is simply talking to God and reminding Him of His words, according to Isaiah 43:26: "Put me in remembrance: let us plead together: declare thou, that thou mayest be justified."

Yes, prayer is another powerful spiritual warfare weapon that will overthrow the enemy of sleeplessness. But there is a correct way in which prayers are to be done because we cannot pray and receive an answer from God if our hearts are filled with iniquities according to Psalm 66:18: "If I regard iniquity in my heart, the Lord will not hear me."

Prayers can be done at any time and anywhere as God's power is not limited to just a church building or a synagogue. Prayers can be made by anyone who has received God's salvation, and it is not limited to only a priest, pope, pastor, bishop, or other religious leaders. Prayers can be done loud or silently without the utterance of any verbal words as God can read the hearts. However, when we pray, we must believe according to the law of Luke 11:24: "Therefore I say unto you, What things soever ye desire, when ye pray, believe that ye receive them, and ye shall have them."

If God's people pray, prayers will heal our various cities, nations, countries, and our world at large. We must pray for God's powerful hands to heal our lands and His will to be done in the world.

> If my people, which are called by my name,
> shall humble themselves, and pray, and seek my
> face, and turn from their wicked ways; then will I
> hear from heaven, and will forgive their sin, and
> will heal their land. (2 Chronicles 7:14)

The truth is, while Christians refuse to pray without ceasing, the witches and the occult world are up praying at various hours from midnight to the early hours before dawn for the evil mandates and will of their master, Satan, to be fulfilled in the lives of the ignorant. No wonder there are so many killings, accidents, and an endless number of diseases and sicknesses in our world. Yes! The wicked pray to Satan (see Deuteronomy 32:17).

So, Paul is reminding us in the law of Ephesians 6:18 that we should make constant prayer and supplication for each other, especially for the saints in Christ. As the prayers of the righteous still heal the sick. Prayer is a powerful weapon that defeats the spirit of infirmity and the enemy of sleeplessness according to the law of James 5.

> And the prayer of faith shall save the sick,
> and the Lord shall raise him up; and if he have
> committed sins, they shall be forgiven him.
> Confess your faults one to another, and pray one

for another, that ye may be healed. The effectual
fervent prayer of a righteous man availeth much.
(James 5:14)

Many people are ignorant of the fact that the encampment
of God's powerful angels around us is also another mighty weapon
against the kingdom of darkness. With God's angels around us, the
enemy of sleeplessness cannot come close to disturbing us from our
sleep as God's ministering angels are there to protect us even while
we sleep. The truth is, we must fear and reverence the Lord in order
for His angels to take up residence around us. No wonder the law
of Psalm 34 reminds us that these angels are there to deliver us who
fear the Lord.

Yes! Another way of overthrowing the evil spirit of sleeplessness
out of our lives is to allow the angels of the Lord to be around us.
God's angels will destroy any demonic spirit who seeks to even come
close to the righteous, as you the righteous are the apples of God's
powerful eyes.

The angels of the Lord encampeth around
about them that fear him, and delivereth them.
(Psalm 34:7)

There is an encampment of God's angels going on right now
around you if you have made Jesus the Christ Lord and Master of
your life. Hence, the evil spirit of sleeplessness has absolutely no legal
rights in your life.

It is clear that spiritual warfare is an ongoing process, and all of
us must be dressed in the armour of God to protect ourselves from
Satan's fiery darts. It is a spiritual fact that to put on or dress in the
armour of God is to walk in obedience to the principles, laws, and
commandments of God. When one is obedient to divine authority,
he or she is dressed in God's armour and ready for battle. The spirit of
sleeplessness can and should be overthrown by using the various warfare weapons outlined in this chapter. But the battle of victory is not
won until one decides to walk in total obedience to God's divine will.

During the years of my oppression, I was up against what the Bible refers to as *this kind* of demon (but I was ignorant at the time) see Matthew 17:21. The demon of sleeplessness is very deceiving and disguising and strives extremely well in the company of his partner, the spirit of ignorance.

The spirit of sleeplessness that was upon me was summoned from an evil altar to carry out his evil mandate in my life. I was ignorant, and I was not dressed in the armour of God; therefore, I was losing the fight. The spirit of sleeplessness had sunken its evil tentacles into my spirit and into my life. He caused years of torture and pain. He was successful with his evil mandate in my life, but all this was because I was ignorant like some of you who might be experiencing this same spirit of sleeplessness and its physical manifestation, even as you are reading this book. It is therefore my desire that the God of Moses will deliver you from the coven of the slave master Pharaoh. I pray that the spirit of sleeplessness will be drowned in the Red Sea of restlessness, according to the law of Matthew 12.

> When the unclean spirit is gone out of a man, he walketh through dry places, seeking rest, and findeth none. (Matthew 12:43)

And when your Pharaoh of sleeplessness is drowned in the sea of restlessness, the songs of victory will gush from your spirits, in the great and powerful name of our Lord and Saviour, Jesus the Christ.

I continued to praise the Lord for my victorious deliverance, I listened at the time to the voice of the Holy Spirit and applied these spiritual principles, now written in this book, and drove out the vicious and evil demonic spirit of sleeplessness, in the name of Jesus.

Today, I continue to walk in the spirit of health and happiness using my story under the leadership of the Holy Spirit and my personal experience to encourage, motivate, and God sets the captives free, in the name of Jesus the Christ.

Witchcraft is an evil spirit that can and must be destroyed with the power of God's Word.

Seven Steps to Drive Out the Evil Spirit of Witchcraft

1. Witchcraft can and should be destroyed with fasting and prayers.

    Howbeit this kind goeth not out but by prayer and fasting. (Matthew 17:21)

2. Witchcraft can and should be destroyed with a constant declaration of the powerful blood of Jesus Christ hidden in your hearts, so you will not sin against God.

    Thy word have I hid in mine heart, That I might not sin against thee. (Psalm 119:11)

    And they overcame him by the blood of the Lamb, and by the word of their testimony; and they loved not their lives unto the death. (Revelation 12:11)

3. Witchcraft can and should be destroyed with a righteous lifestyle as defined in the scriptures.

    Because it is written, Be ye holy; for I am holy. (1 Peter 1:16)

4. Witchcraft can and should be destroyed by using the spirit of forgiveness.

    For if ye forgive men their trespasses, your heavenly Father will also forgive you; But if ye forgive not men their trespasses, neither will your Father forgive your trespasses. (Matthew 6:14–15)

5. Witchcraft can and should be destroyed with the spirit of knowledge.

> Study to shew thyself approved unto God, a workman that needeth not to be ashamed, rightly dividing the word of truth. (2 Timothy 2:15)

> But through knowledge shall the just be delivered. (Proverbs 11:9b)

6. Witchcraft can and should be destroyed with the sword of the spirit. Hebrews 4:12 says,

> For the word of God is alive and active. Sharper than any double-edged sword, it penetrates even to dividing soul and spirit, joints and marrow; it judges the thoughts and attitudes of the heart.

7. Witchcraft can and should be destroyed with the spirit of prayers and thanksgiving unto God.

> Pray without ceasing. In everything give thanks: for this is the will of God in Christ Jesus concerning you. (1 Thessalonians 5:17–18)

> Praying always with all prayer and supplication in the Spirit, and watching thereunto with all perseverance and supplication for all saints. (Ephesians 6:18)

It is only with a life of total obedience that we can truly destroy the spirit of witchcraft that is set against our lives. There is no other way but the way of the cross. Rebellion to the principles of God also falls under the sin of witchcraft, and Satan cannot cast out Satan.

> For rebellion is as the sin of witchcraft, and stubbornness is as iniquity and idolatry. Because thou hast rejected the word of the LORD, he hath also rejected thee from being king. (1 Samuel 15:23)

It is totally impossible for any of us to bind and cast out demonic spirits if we are not walking in total obedience to the law of God. When we examine Acts 19, we read about the consequences of going up against an unclean spirit with an unrighteous lifestyle. If you are a child of the devil, do not attempt to bind and cast him out because you will be bound and cast down with multiple problems, and your situation(s) will be seven times greater than what it was. Spiritual warfare is not a copycat business; it is rather a deep-rooted spiritual battle between good (God) and evil (Satan). Moreover, you must be on the side of the Lord to win.

> And God wrought special miracles by the hands of Paul: So that from his body were brought unto the sick handkerchiefs or aprons, and the diseases departed from them, and the evil spirits went out of them. Then certain of the vagabond Jews, exorcists, took upon them to call over them which had evil spirits the name of the Lord Jesus, saying, We adjure you by Jesus whom Paul preacheth. And there were seven sons of one Sceva, a Jew, and chief of the priests, which did so. And the evil spirit answered and said, Jesus, I know, and Paul I know; but who are ye? And the man in whom the evil spirit was leaped on them, and overcame them, and prevailed against them, so that they fled out of that house naked and wounded. (Acts 19:11–16) (see also Matthew 12:26)

CHAPTER 6

The Power of the Tongue

Warfare is fought through the power of the mouth gate. We must therefore use our tongue to speak the Word of God against the demon of our sleep. We must then locate all the spiritual laws and promises that talk about sleep, health, and the victory we have over the works of the enemy, in the name of Jesus Christ.

When we look at the book of Proverbs, it warns us about the power of our words. This is because we shall have whatever it is that we are saying, as life and death still reside in the power of our individual tongues as stated in the law of Proverbs 18 below.

> Death and life are in the power of the tongue: and they that love it shall eat the fruit thereof. (Proverbs 18:21)

We must understand that our words are spirits and they are life. Our words have the ability to produce blessings as well as curses. They can break into pieces, and they can make whole. Our words can bring healing as well as invoke sickness and diseases depending on whose words we are speaking. God will make sure that He watches over His words to perform them in our lives. It is in the book of Matthew that we get a very close-up encounter with the Word of God, who is Jesus, the Son of God, reminding the devil of the written Word as Satan seeks to release the spirit of temptation. "Jesus said unto him, It is written again, Thou shalt not tempt the Lord thy God" (Matthew 4:7). Jesus spoke the Word consistently because the Word is the powerful weapon that brings about deliverance. Let us go deep because the word of God kills and makes alive. It destroys demons, devils, and the entire kingdom of Satan. But it also washes us and makes us alive in Christ.

> It is the spirit that quickeneth; the flesh profiteth nothing: the words that I speak unto you, they are spirit, and they are life. (John 6:63)

There are several scriptural references in the Holy Bible that talk about the words of our mouths.

It is in the book of Hebrews that we understand the principle and the power of the spoken Word because it is through this powerful law, that we see that it is the Word of God that creates everything, including the universe. The word of God spoken in the invisible brings manifestation to the visible. This is powerful as it is teaching us a very important spiritual lesson that will aid us as we slay our Goliaths of sickness, hardships, sleeplessness, and the like.

It is a spiritual fact that the Word when spoken in faith will preserve our lives as it directs our path to righteousness (see also Psalm 119:105).

> Through faith we understand that the worlds were framed by the word of God, so that things which are seen were not made of things which do appear. (Hebrews 11:3)

We must, therefore, use the word of God as a spiritual weapon against the enemy of our destiny. It is Jeremiah the prophet who opens our spiritual eyes to the fact that God's Word is like a hammer that breaketh the rocks of failure, destruction, poverty, sickness, and the spirit of sleeplessness into pieces out of your life in Jesus' name. In addition, the word is like a fire that will burn and destroy these broken pieces. We should put the powerful Word of God on the tips of our tongues, march out on the battlefield of life and wage war on the enemy in the name of Jesus. We can send the blood of Jesus to every evil altar, coven, and anywhere in the invisible and visible worlds by the power of our tongues. We can also call down the Holy Ghost fire upon every evil altar and evil sacrifice that is lifted against our sleep by the power of our tongues in the name of Jesus. Our tongues are powerful and you shall have that which you are saying according to Mark 11, "Therefore, I say unto you, What things soever ye desire, when ye pray, believe that ye receive them, and ye shall have them" (Mark 11:24).

When we use our tongues the way God intended for them to be used, we are doing powerful spiritual warfare against the invisible world and against the demon of sleeplessness. For it is written,

> A man's belly shall be satisfied with the fruit
> of his mouth: and with the increase of his lips
> shall he be filled. (Proverbs 18:20)

If you start using the powerful sword of the spirit (God's word) to command the elements of creation, to locate the enemy of your sleep and fight, then you will be victorious in your warfare against the enemy.

The warfare principle was first used by the Word Himself, Jesus Christ. Jesus uses the power of his tongue with God's Word to defeat the spirits of sickness, poverty, witchcraft, and every other unclean spirit that shows up in His presence, including the spirit of death.

> And when he thus had spoken, he cried
> with a loud voice, Lazarus, come forth. And he
> that was dead came forth, bound hand and foot
> with graveclothes: and his face was bound about
> with a napkin. Jesus saith unto them, loose him,
> and let him go. (John 11:43–44)

It is a spiritual fact according to the law of Genesis 1:26–28 that man has full dominion over God's creation when he speaks God's Word in faith and obedience.

> And God said, Let us make man in our image, after our likeness: and let them have dominion over the fish of the sea, and over the fowl of the air, and over the cattle, and over all the earth, and over every creeping thing that creepeth upon the earth.
>
> So God created man in his own image, in the image of God created he him; male and female created he them.
>
> And God blessed them, and God said unto them, Be fruitful, and multiply, and replenish the earth, and subdue it: and have dominion over the fish of the sea, and over the fowl of the air, and over every living thing that moveth upon the earth. (Genesis 1:26–28)

We witness Deborah, an Old Testament prophetess, under the anointing of God's power activate this authority, as she used the sword of the Spirit, the Word of God, and commanded the stars to fight against the enemy, *Sisera*, according to Judges 5.

> They fought from heaven; the stars in their courses fought against Sisera. (Judges 5:20)

And in Joshua 10:13, we witness Joshua using the same spiritual principles, as he uses the power of his tongue, to command the sun to stand still so that he can have total victory over the enemies.

> And the sun stood still, and the moon stayed, until the people had avenged themselves upon their enemies. Is not this written in the book of Jasher? So the sun stood still in the midst

73

of heaven, and hasted not to go down about a
whole day. (Joshua 10:13)

All throughout the Scriptures, we see men and women of God
on the invisible battlefield, using the power of their tongues to engage
in powerful spiritual warfare with the enemy and his agents.

Elijah, the Tishbite, closed up the heavens with the power of
his tongue. It was more than just a drought; it was a spiritual warfare
between the powers of good and the powers of evil.

Elias was a man subject to like passions as
we are, and he prayed earnestly that it might not
rain: and it rained not on the earth by the space
of three years and six months. (James 5:17)

True believers in Jesus Christ have power and authority over all
demonic powers and spirits, including the spirit of sleeplessness, in
the mighty name of Jesus.

Behold, I give unto you power to tread on
serpents and scorpions, and over all the power of
the enemy: and nothing shall by any means hurt
you. (Luke 10:19)

The Spirit of Praise on the Tongues of the Believers

The tongues of the believers should be coated with the spirit
of praise and used as a powerful warfare weapon against the enemy;
the enemy of sleeplessness. It is in the book of 2 Chronicles that we
witness the effect of a powerful ambushment as the powerful warfare
weapons of praise and worship, was activated by King Jehoshaphat
and the Israelites against their enemies.

As Jehoshaphat and the Israelites marched upon the battlefield with powerful songs and praises unto God, their enemies were

defeated, and Jehoshaphat and his people walked away with an abundance of blessings.

The Bible also declared that Jehoshaphat experienced peace and rest all around him for the rest of his life. The weapon of praise and worship will no doubt destroy the enemy of your sleep and give you rest. See the story below of what the power of the tongue can do for the believers of Jesus the Christ.

> And they rose early in the morning, and went forth into the wilderness of Tekoa: and as they went forth, Jehoshaphat stood and said, Hear me, O Judah, and ye inhabitants of Jerusalem; Believe in the LORD your God, so shall ye be established; believe his prophets, so shall ye prosper.
>
> And when he had consulted with the people, he appointed singers unto the LORD, and that should praise the beauty of holiness, as they went out before the army, and to say, Praise the LORD; for his mercy endureth for ever.
>
> And when they began to sing and to praise, the LORD set ambushments against the children of Ammon, Moab, and mount Seir, which were come against Judah; and they were smitten.
>
> For the children of Ammon and Moab stood up against the inhabitants of mount Seir, utterly to slay and destroy them: and when they had made an end of the inhabitants of Seir, every one helped to destroy another.
>
> And when Judah came toward the watch tower in the wilderness, they looked unto the multitude, and, behold, they were dead bodies fallen to the earth, and none escaped.
>
> And when Jehoshaphat and his people came to take away the spoil of them, they found among them in abundance both riches with the dead

bodies, and precious jewels, which they stripped off for themselves, more than they could carry away: and they were three days in gathering of the spoil, it was so much."

And on the fourth day they assembled themselves in the valley of Berachah; for there they blessed the LORD: therefore the name of the same place was called, The valley of Berachah, unto this day.

Then they returned, every man of Judah and Jerusalem, and Jehoshaphat in the forefront of them, to go again to Jerusalem with joy; for the LORD had made them to rejoice over their enemies.

And they came to Jerusalem with psalteries and harps and trumpets unto the house of the LORD.

And the fear of God was on all the kingdoms of those countries, when they had heard that the LORD fought against the enemies of Israel.

So the realm of Jehoshaphat was quiet: for his God gave him rest round about. (2 Chronicles 20:21–30)

You can and should defeat your enemy of sleeplessness or your Pharaoh of sleeplessness by using the power of your tongue. Fill your mouth with the powerful Word of God as you sing and praise His high and holy name, and the enemy of sleeplessness will be drowned in the red sea of confusion in the name of Jesus.

And Moses said unto the people, Fear ye not, stand still, and see the salvation of the LORD, which he will shew to you to day: for the Egyptians whom ye have seen to day, ye shall see them again no more forever. (Exodus 14:13)

David, a man after God's own heart, showed us exactly how warfare is done, as he used his mouth to first defeat the enemy, and later the manifestation of this defeat occurred in the physical. The powerful Goliath of Gath was seen without a head. David cut off the enemy's head first in the spirit and then in the physical. This is how we are to fight our Goliath of sleeplessness, as seen in the narrative below.

> Then said David to the Philistine, Thou comest to me with a sword, and with a spear, and with a shield: but I come to thee in the name of the LORD of hosts, the God of the armies of Israel, whom thou hast defied. This day the LORD will deliver you into my hands, and I'll strike you down and cut off your head. This very day I will give the carcasses of the Philistine army to the birds and the wild animals, and the whole world will know that there is a God in Israel. All those gathered here will know that it is not by sword or spear that the LORD saves; for the battle is the LORD's, and he will give all of you into our hands. As the Philistine moved closer to attack him, David ran quickly toward the battle line to meet him. Reaching into his bag and taking out a stone, he slung it and struck the Philistine on the forehead. The stone sank into his forehead, and he fell face down on the ground. So David triumphed over the Philistine with a sling and a stone; without a sword in his hand he struck down the Philistine and killed him.
>
> David ran and stood over him. He took hold of the Philistine's sword and drew it from the sheath. After he killed him, he cut off his head with the sword. (1 Samuel 17:45–50)

As believers, we too must learn how to use our warfare sword and cut off the head of the enemy of sleeplessness. We must remember that it is a life of obedience, saturated with praise and worship, fasting, and prayer, the dress code of righteousness, the spirit of knowledge, saturated with the Word of the Lord, and a repentant heart all wrapped up in the powerful victorious blood of Jesus the Christ, that will leave our Goliaths of sleeplessness in a headless situation.

When a decreeing tongue is wrapped up with the powerful blood of Jesus Christ, our enemies get nervous. The enemies of the evil altars—witchcraft, sleeplessness—cannot stand in the presence of a decreeing tongue as anything can happen, according to the law of Job 22.

> Thou shalt also decree a thing, and it shall be established unto thee. (Job 22:28)

However, it is sad that many times, we allow the enemy and his agents to use the powerful weapon of our warfare against us. The witches and the witchcraft practitioners are the ones who are using the power of their evil tongues to shuttle many into captivities of sicknesses, hardships, chaos, restlessness, sleeplessness, and even premature death. It is a fact that power has shifted hand and God's people are perishing, as highlighted in Isaiah 5 below

> Therefore my people are gone into captivity, because they have no knowledge: and their honourable men are famished, and their multitude dried up with thirst. (Isaiah 5:13)

Yes, many of God's people are clueless as to how important the words that are coming from their mouths are. Oftentimes, many engage in idle conversations such as gossiping and backbiting. But the Bible warns us that we will have to stand before God and give an account for the time we spend in these sinful and unprofitable practices.

We should become knowledgeable of the fact that when we practice speaking evil, we are inviting demons into our spirits, and we are no better than the witches.

It is also wise for us to know that in the very same way, we are using our tongues against the enemy, the witches are also chanting with their evil tongues against the Christians as they send out spirits of sicknesses, diseases, accidents, poverty, and deaths in our world.

So, at no point in time should you allow your tongue to speak evil.

> An evil tongue can kill a spirit and break a heart.

As mentioned throughout the chapters of this book, it is with our mouths and a spirit of obedience to divine authority that we fight spiritual warfare. Therefore, it is very important that the powerful Word of the Lord is on the tips of our tongues. It is no coincidence that the law of Ephesians 4 reminds us about our conversations.

> Let no corrupt communication proceed out of your mouth, but that which is good to the use of edifying, that it may minister grace unto the hearers. (Ephesians 4:29)

So, let us be strong and courageous like our God, as we use the power of our tongues to create, destroy and restore, just like Him, in the name of Jesus.

> Be strong and courageous, be not afraid nor dismayed for the king of Assyria, nor for all the multitude that *is* with him: for *there be* more with us than with him. (2 Chronicles 32:7)

CHAPTER 7

The Blood of Jesus as a Spiritual Warfare Weapon

When we look at the powerful blood of Jesus the Christ and how important it is to both the invisible and the visible worlds, we would be amazingly grateful for His precious blood. The blood of Jesus is the all-powerful one-time payment for all and every sin of mankind. The Bible clearly states that without the shedding of blood, there is no remission for any of our sins (see Hebrews 9:22).

It is a spiritual fact that the life of all flesh is in the blood; therefore, Christ had to become flesh but without sin to save us through the shedding of His blood. It is the blood of Jesus that makes atonement for our souls. The blood is important because, without it, we would not have forgiveness to gain eternal life. The blood of Jesus the Christ is the defensive weapon against all forms of evil sacrifices, evil decrees, and demonic blood that are speaking against you and your health, including your sleep.

Anyone who accepts the powerful blood of Jesus automatically accepts life and has the legal God-given right to enter into eternity with God. The powerful blood of Jesus has the divine power to not only give life but to sustain life. As a matter of fact, the law of Acts 17:28 clearly states that it is in Him that we live, move, and have our being. Anyone with the mark of His blood on him also has God's approval to also use His blood as a warfare weapon against the kingdom of darkness, and its works. The powerful blood of Jesus is the only weapon against Satan and his kingdom.

It is the blood of Jesus that breaks the shackles and sets the captives free.

It heals, protects, assures, and gives eternal life to all those who dare to plead it in righteousness.

The blood of Jesus is a covenant between God and man. However, those who do not accept Jesus as their personal saviour from sin do not have any legal right to plead His blood or to call upon it because it will work against them.

The powerful speaking blood of Jesus should be decreed and declared over your life, health, home, family, and all that is connected to you, in Jesus' name. It will destroy and loosen the bands of wickedness, undo heavy burdens, and make the oppressed go free while breaking every demonic yoke that is spiritually tied around your destiny.

Every believer in Jesus has the legal right to use His powerful victorious blood as a weapon against the evil spirit of infirmity, witchcraft, torment, restlessness, sleeplessness, and the like. Neither Satan nor his works can stand in the way or the path of the blood. Remember, it is the blood that overcame him and his kingdom as outlined in the powerful law of Revelation 12 below.

> And they overcame him by the blood of
> the Lamb, and by the word of their testimony;
> and they loved not their lives unto the death.
> (Revelation 12:11)

By now, we should be knowledgeable of the fact that the spirit of sleeplessness is a witchcraft spirit, and he is an invisible being from the kingdom of Satan. We should also be knowledgeable that this evil spirit, like all the others, comes to kill, steal, and destroy our lives and our divine destinies. Therefore, we must stop him by using the powerful blood of Jesus the Christ as a weapon.

The blood of Jesus not only delivers and sets captives free, but it also speaks and oppresses the oppressors, in the name of Jesus. It will paralyze the enemy of sleeplessness if you know how to apply it.

The blood of Jesus the Christ can also be used as a judgment of woe against the wicked: hence, it is therefore important to send the blood of Jesus into every secret, visible and invisible, coven and cauldron where your name has been called for evil. The spirit of witchcraft must start eating his own flesh and drinking his own blood (see Isaiah 49:26). Let us go deeper because you who are captives by the evil spirit of sleeplessness, must engage in powerful warfare sessions of prayer and plead the blood of Jesus against the spirit of witchcraft. You must burn their habitations and their spiritual transportation system. You must use the blood of Jesus to dismantle their network. Many times, it is household witchcraft that is public enemy number one in our lives. Someone within the family or some close acquaintances who seek to allow Satan to use them as the vessels of destruction against us. Therefore, when we fight "spiritually" using the blood of Jesus, we should have absolutely no mercy on household witchcraft. We must send the blood of Jesus wrapped around the sword of the Spirit and destroy their operation. Likewise, you should reverse all witchcraft burial against your sleep, health, and life and break their curses in the name of Jesus.

It is important to know that we should also come against their evil thrones while we possess the gates of the enemies using the blood of Jesus. Show absolutely no mercy in rendering the evil spirit of witchcraft and its curses powerless in your life and that of your family.

Finally, we should set their covens and their evil caldrons on fire because as stated in the text below, witchcraft city shall not be your caldron.

> This city shall not be your caldron, neither shall ye be the flesh in the midst thereof; but I will judge you in the border of Israel. (Ezekiel 11:11)

The powerful blood of Jesus as a spiritual weapon against the evil spirit of sleeplessness should be sprinkled at every T-junction, crossroads, and everywhere there are visible and invisible evil altars of demonic blood sacrifices against your life and destiny, in the name of Jesus.

Let us remember that there is life in the blood, and the blood of Jesus the Christ is the ultimate sacrificial blood that overcomes all other blood. It is still speaking even today, and it will answer the evil voices that are set against your sleep and your health if you know how to send it to the evil altars in His name.

> For the life of the flesh is in the blood: and I have given it to you upon the altar to make an atonement for your souls: for it is the blood that maketh an atonement for the soul. (Leviticus 17:11)

It is a spiritual fact according to Scriptures, that the enemies we see today we shall see them no more because they will die in our stead.

> The righteous is delivered out of trouble, and the wicked cometh in his stead. (Proverbs 11:8)

The Blood of Jesus Against the Spirit of Jealousy

According to Ezekiel chapter 8, the spirit of jealousy is an abomination unto God, and God is against it. When we carefully analyze Ezekiel's vision in chapter 8 of Ezekiel, we get a clearer description of this spirit, and we also see the wrath of God played out in chapter 9 of the text. The spirit of jealousy causes the glory of God to depart from the house of Israel and from the sanctuary as can be seen in the narrative here below.

> Then said he unto me, Son of man, lift up thine eyes now the way toward the north. So I lifted up mine eyes the way toward the north,

> and behold northward at the gate of the altar this image of jealousy in the entry. He said furthermore unto me, Son of man, seest thou what they do? even the great abominations that the house of Israel committeth here, that I should go far off from my sanctuary? but turn thee yet again, and thou shalt see greater abominations. (Ezekiel 8:5–6)

The spirit of jealousy, like all the other evil spirits from the kingdom of darkness, should be fought using the powerful, victorious blood of Jesus. The Bible is clear in Revelation 12:11 that it is by the blood of Jesus that we defeat the works of darkness.

Jealousy is a dangerous and deadly spirit that comes from Satan, and anyone in whom this spirit is found is a captive of his. It is also a witchcraft spirit, that calls for blood.

The witchcraft spirit of jealousy is rampant, it is within our churches among leaders, pastors, and many who call themselves Christians. Sad, but it is also true that this spirit of jealousy has made its way into many bedrooms between husbands and their wives as highlighted in the law of Numbers 5 below and, by extension, the rest of the family. Satan does come to kill, steal, and destroy homes, families, lives, and destinies.

> And the spirit of jealousy come upon him, and he be jealous of his wife, and she be defiled: or if the spirit of jealousy come upon him, and he be jealous of his wife, and she be not defiled. (Numbers 5:14)

From the Scriptures, we have witnessed this same spirit of jealousy enter the spirit of Cain and cause him to kill his brother Abel. This spirit is still roaming about, seeking whom he may devour. He fights against brothers and sisters and causes conflicts in homes, in marriages, in the workplace, and in our world at large. No doubt he is a spiritual murderer.

> Whosoever hateth his brother is a murderer:
> and ye know that no murderer hath eternal life
> abiding in him. (1 John 3:15)

Many people have been murdered spiritually and physically because of the danger of this evil witchcraft spirit. But the sad thing about it is that he is getting away with his evil because only a few with spiritual eyesight can see him.

As the Holy Spirit opened my eyes to the story of Cain and Abel, the earth's first family, I began to understand how deadly of a spirit jealousy is. He does not think twice, and he is super vicious; after all, he is a blood drinker and a flesh eater. He is an oppressor, a robber, a destroyer and a killer; so do not be deceived. Here in the narrative below, we witness for ourselves the spirit of jealousy at work in the life of Cain the captive. But let us, as we read this story, search our own lives and see if this evil being also lives within us because God will be asking us the very same question he asked Cain. Remember, we should be our brother's keeper!

> And in process of time it came to pass, that
> Cain brought of the fruit of the ground an offer-
> ing unto the Lord. And Abel, he also brought of
> the firstlings of his flock and of the fat thereof.
> And the Lord had respect unto Abel and to his
> offering: But unto Cain and to his offering he
> had not respect. And Cain was very wroth, and
> his countenance fell. And the Lord said unto
> Cain, Why art thou wroth? and why is thy coun-
> tenance fallen? If thou doest well, shalt thou not
> be accepted? and if thou doest not well, sin lieth
> at the door. And unto thee shall be his desire,
> and thou shalt rule over him. And Cain talked
> with Abel his brother: and it came to pass, when

they were in the field, that Cain rose up against Abel his brother, and slew him. And the Lord said unto Cain, Where is Abel thy brother? And he said, I know not: Am I my brother's keeper? (Genesis 4:3–9)

God Uses the Evil of the Enemies to Catapult the Righteous

The Bible continues to speak in several Scriptures that a man's foe is that of his household, as we have already witnessed in two narratives within this chapter. The life of Joseph comes to remind us that even though many of us are believers and faithful followers of Jesus, the witchcraft spirit of jealousy can still attack us if we fail to see him for who he is. Therefore, let us stop looking at the physical appearance of a man and start looking at the spirit that governs the man. This way the spirit of jealousy will be exposed and prayerfully will be destroyed with the powerful blood of Jesus.

The narrative in Genesis 37 opens our spiritual eyes to the behavior of this evil spirit. Because, like Joseph, you don't have to provoke this evil spirit; all you need to do for him to show his wicked self is for you to look promising. Jealousy is troubled by the favor of God in a person's life. He hates progress, and he will do just about anything to stop you, including drinking your blood if you let him. Joseph's brothers, who hosted the spirit of jealousy, saw the divine anointing of favor that was upon Joseph's life; and they wanted to destroy it. But they could not have destroyed the favor without destroying Joseph, but the thing about God's favor upon our lives is that even if the enemies kill us, they cannot take that favor. As a matter of fact, the curses of God will be doubled even more upon them and their seeds that try to take His favor away from us. God, through His permissive will, allows the evil spirit of jealousy to carry out his evil mandate in Joseph's life with the exception of killing him. The spirit of jealousy could not kill Joseph because God had a perfect plan for the fulfillment of the promise He made to Abraham and his seed through Joseph's life.

> And it came to pass, when Joseph was come unto his brethren, that they stript Joseph out of his coat, his coat of many colours that was on him; and they took him, and cast him into a pit: and the pit was empty, there was no water in it. And they sat down to eat bread: and they lifted up their eyes and looked, and, behold, a company of Ishmeelites came from Gilead with their camels bearing spicery and balm and myrrh, going to carry it down to Egypt. And Judah said unto his brethren, What profit is it if we slay our brother, and conceal his blood? Come, and let us sell him to the Ishmeelites, and let not our hand be upon him; for he is our brother and our flesh. And his brethren were content. Then there passed by Midianites merchantmen; and they drew and lifted up Joseph out of the pit, and sold Joseph to the Ishmeelites for twenty pieces of silver: and they brought Joseph into Egypt. (Geneses 37:23–28)

Jealousy cannot kill our great destiny in Jesus as it is God who has the final say in all things, and who He blesses, no man curses as proclaimed by Balaam the Sorcerer in Numbers 23:8. However, at times I question, "Why God allowed Able to die?" But then the Holy Spirit answered and told me, "If Abel had not died, the marks of destruction would not be placed on all those who allowed the spirit of jealousy to use them as weapons against the righteous." Moreover, Abel will be sure to make it to God's eternal kingdom, but Cain cannot and will not.

As was said earlier, the spirit of jealousy will make its way into any life that is not covered by the blood of Jesus. It is the blood of Jesus that shields us from evil. Therefore, one must walk in the spirit of obedience to be protected by the blood. When we look at how close to Jesus the spirit of jealousy walked, now we know that he is not a pushover. Judas, the betrayer, even though physically walking and moving alongside Jesus and the rest of the disciples, was engulfed by a spirit of jealousy. But having studied Judas' life, I also understood that he had numerous evil spirits living within him even while serving as a disciple of Jesus. Judas was a case by himself because the spirit of stupidity must have been his twin brother. How could you want to hide your mind from the God who knows all things, Judas? The love and greed for material things placed a deadly burden upon the shoulders of Judas, and in split seconds, his spiritual eyesight was no more. He betrayed the master out of a heart of greed and jealousy as can be witnessed in the narrative of Matthew here below.

> And while he yet spake, lo, Judas, one of the twelve, came, and with him a great multitude with swords and staves, from the chief priests and elders of the people. Now he that betrayed him gave them a sign, saying, Whomsoever I shall kiss, that same is he: hold him fast. And forthwith he came to Jesus, and said, Hail, master; and kissed him. And Jesus said unto him, Friend, wherefore art thou come? Then came they, and laid hands on Jesus and took him. (Matthew 26:47–50)

Great men and women of God have been victims of the evil witchcraft spirit of jealousy, but God continues to use this enemy as a stepping stone to our divine destinies.

Even in the life of Daniel, we also observed that the spirit of jealousy was sent against him even though he was a faithful man who prayed three times per day.

However, the lives of the wicked are always a substitute for the righteous, as we can witness in the story of Daniel. Even though Daniel was attacked by the evil spirit of jealousy and was thrown into the lion's den, he was in perfect peace. The victorious and powerful hands of the almighty God kept Daniel safe. The angels of the Lord closed the mouths of the lions, and the haters of Daniel along with their families died instead of Daniel. Daniel chapter 6 is also a powerful example of many of our lives, both the haters and the righteous. The haters will continue to hate, and eventually, they will fall into their own traps. We, the righteous, will have the peace that passes all understanding to be our strength in facing our lion's dens. God will never leave nor forsake us, the apples of His loving eyes. As you read this powerful narrative of Daniel 6, your spiritual eyes will begin to open and you will see that the spirit of jealousy is a selfish, evil witchcraft spirit that comes to kill, steal, and destroy lives and destinies. He is brutal and deadly. He only uses and abuses his victims; and in the end, you, the foolish who allowed him in, will pay the great and dreadful price of destruction. The enemies of Daniel and their ignorant families ended up becoming the victims of their own conspiracy.

> And over these three presidents; of whom Daniel was first: that the princes might give accounts unto them, and the king should have no damage. Then this Daniel was preferred above the presidents and princes, because an excellent spirit was in him; and the king thought to set him over the whole realm. Then the presidents and princes sought to find occasion against Daniel concerning the kingdom; but they could find none occasion nor fault; forasmuch as he was faithful, neither was there any error or fault found in him. Then said these men, We shall not find any occasion against this Daniel, except we find it against him concerning the law of his God. Then these presidents and princes assembled together to the king, and said thus unto him, King Darius, live forever. All the presidents of the kingdom, the governors, and the princes, the counsellors, and the captains, have consulted together to establish a royal statute, and to make a firm decree, that whosoever shall ask a petition of any God or man for thirty days, save of thee, O king, he shall be cast into the den of

lions. Now, O king, establish the decree, and sign the writing, that it be not changed, according to the law of the Medes and Persians, which altereth not. Wherefore king Darius signed the writing and the decree. Now when Daniel knew that the writing was signed, he went into his house; and his windows being open in his chamber toward Jerusalem, he kneeled upon his knees three times a day, and prayed, and gave thanks before his God, as he did aforetime. Then these men assembled, and found Daniel praying and making supplication before his God. Then they came near, and spake before the king concerning the king's decree; Hast thou not signed a decree, that every man that shall ask a petition of any God or man within thirty days, save of thee, O king, shall be cast into the den of lions? The king answered and said, The thing is true, according to the law of the Medes and Persians, which altereth not. Then answered they and said before the king, That Daniel, which is of the children of the captivity of Judah, regardeth not thee, O king, nor the decree that thou hast signed, but maketh his petition three times a day. Then the king, when he heard these words, was sore displeased with himself, and set his heart on Daniel to deliver him: and he laboured till the going down of the sun to deliver him. Then these men assembled unto the king, and said unto the king, Know, O king, that the law of the Medes and Persians is, That no decree nor statute which the king establisheth may be changed. Then the king commanded, and they brought Daniel, and cast him into the den of lions. Now the king spake and said unto Daniel, Thy God whom thou servest continually, he will deliver thee. And a stone was brought, and laid upon the mouth of the den; and the king sealed it with his own signet, and with the signet of his lords; that the purpose might not be changed concerning Daniel. Then the king went to his palace, and passed the night fasting: neither were instruments of music brought before him: and his sleep went from him. Then the king arose very early in the morning, and went in haste unto the den of lions. And when he came to the den, he cried with a lamentable voice unto Daniel: and the king spake and said to Daniel, O Daniel, servant of the living God, is thy God, whom thou servest continually, able to deliver thee from the lions? Then said Daniel unto the king, O king, live for ever. My God hath sent his angel, and hath shut the lions' mouths, that they have not hurt me: forasmuch as before him innocency was found in me; and also before thee, O king, have I done no hurt. Then was the king exceedingly glad for him, and commanded that they should take Daniel up out of the den. So Daniel was taken up out of the den, and no manner of hurt was found upon him, because he believed in his God. And the king commanded, and they brought those men which had accused Daniel, and they cast them into the den of lions, them, their children, and their wives; and the lions had the mastery of them, and brake all their bones in pieces or ever they came at the bottom of the den.

Then king Darius wrote unto all people, nations, and languages, that dwell in all the earth; Peace be multiplied unto you.

I make a decree, That in every dominion of my kingdom men tremble and fear before the God of Daniel: for he is the living God, and steadfast for ever, and his kingdom that which shall not be destroyed, and his dominion shall be even unto the end.

He delivereth and rescueth, and he worketh
signs and wonders in heaven and in earth, who
hath delivered Daniel from the power of the lions.

So this Daniel prospered in the reign of
Darius, and in the reign of Cyrus the Persian.
(Daniel 6:2–28)

I have to keep referring to my story because the spirit of jealousy
was also the vessel that was used against my life. Satan and his agents
hate to see you climbing the ladder of success, and the witchcraft spirit of
jealousy is always available to do the dirty work of trying to hijack your
life and destiny. But for persons, including myself, who will be radical
enough and tell the devil that enough is enough, they will be catapulted
into even greater success or good success according to Joshaua 1:8b.

It is the powerful blood of Jesus the Christ that will bind every
strong man and woman of sleeplessness and set you the captive free
as He has done for me many years ago. The spiritual laws of Mark
and Luke teach us the spiritual principles of binding and casting out
demons and devils in the name of Jesus. God wants us to know that
we have the legal right to bind up the witchcraft spirit of jealousy that
is set against many of our lives. When this spirit is bound, his works
are also bound up and he cannot prosper against us.

No man can enter into a strong man's
house, and spoil his goods, except he will first
bind the strong man; and then he will spoil his
house. (Mark 3:27)

The blood of Jesus the Christ will cut your sleep out of the
hands of the wicked witches and allow you to enjoy sweet, deep,
healthy sleep again if you know how to plead His blood.

And I will cut off witchcrafts out of thine
hand; and thou shalt have no *more* soothsayers.
(Micah 5:12)

It is the blood of Jesus the Christ when plead in righteousness that will bring total restoration to your life, including your sleep and health.

> Beloved, I wish above all things that thou mayest prosper and be in health, even as thy soul prospereth. (3 John 2)

The truth is, the blood of Jesus makes sure that the evil counsel of the wicked against your sleep will not stand nor come to pass.

> Take counsel together, and it shall come to nought; speak the word, and it shall not stand: for God is with us. (Isaiah 8:10)

The blood has already disarmed, disemboweled, and destroyed the works of the enemies against your life.

> And having spoiled principalities and powers, he made a shew of them openly, triumphing over the them in it. (Colossians 2:15s)

It was the divine knowledge of the Holy Spirit that guided me and gave me victory over the demon of sleeplessness that had tormented me for several years.

I had to learn how to undo all the lies of the enemy. I had to use the powerful blood of Jesus the Christ to wash out my spirit so that His Holy Spirit could rest and abide with me. The yoke of God had to be upon my life for me to find that rest for my soul, as narrated in Matthew 11.

> Take my yoke upon you, and learn of me; for I am meek and lowly in heart: and ye shall find rest unto your souls. (Matthew 11:29)

The blood of Jesus is an antidote against sin. It fights sins, and absolutely no form, shape, or size of sin can exist under the blood of Jesus. With that said, it is therefore impossible for one to be practicing any form of secret or open sins and still insist on pleading the blood.

Many people will never receive their miracles because they are trying to plead the blood only when they are in the house of worship and in the presence of pastors, bishops, elders, or leaders.

The blood of Jesus when handled with a righteous hand will bring about deliverance, and it will stop all the demonic weapons that are forming against your sleep, in the name of Jesus the Christ.

> No weapon that is formed against thee shall prosper; and every tongue that shall rise against thee in judgment thou shalt condemn. This is the heritage of the servants of the LORD, and their righteousness is of me, saith the LORD. (Isaiah 54:17)

I must remind us that it is important to maintain our deliverance because it is not that the demonic weapons are not forming; but if we continue to be covered under the blood, then as stated in the law of Isaiah 54:17, these weapons of destruction shall not prosper as they would have had no legal grounds on which to take any effect. The Lord shall keep us who are marked by His blood under His wings as declared in the law of Psalm 91 below. So let us seek daily to maintain our deliverance in the name of Jesus.

> He shall cover thee with his feathers, and under his wings shalt thou trust: his truth shall be thy shield and buckler. Thou shalt not be afraid for the terror by night; nor for the arrow that flieth by day. (Psalm 91:4–5)

CHAPTER 8

Maintaining Your Deliverance

Friends, the enemy of sleeplessness can and will return if you are not walking in the spirit of obedience to God's divine law. It is obedience to the voice of God that keeps evil spirits out of our lives (see John 14:15–23).

The Bible in Matthew 12 tells us that if an evil spirit is cast out of a person's life, that person is delivered. However, if he is not maintaining his deliverance, then that evil spirit along with more wicked spirits will gain entrance back into the life of that person.

> When the unclean spirit is gone out of a man, he walketh through dry places, seeking rest, and findeth none. Then he saith, I will return into my house from whence I came out; and when he is come, he findeth it empty, swept, and garnished. (Matthew 12:43–44)

But what is deliverance and how to maintain our deliverance as this, too, is of vital importance for our Christian journey? Deliverance, according to the Scriptures, is the spiritual knowledge and understanding along with the application of it to our lives that causes us to take on the mind of Jesus the Christ. In order for one to maintain his deliverance, he must continue to study the Word of God and make it applicable to his life (see Proverbs 11:9).

Deliverance is a spiritual process that starts with learning. When we are aware of the truth about our real enemies—Satan and his demons, and the number one ammunition that they use on the battlefield—we are well on our way to becoming victorious in this warfare.

> And ye shall know the truth, and the truth
> shall make you free. (John 8:32)

We maintain our deliverance by consistently walking in the truth, who is Jesus the Christ, as stated in John 8, also John 14.

> Jesus saith unto him, I am the way, the truth,
> and the life: no man cometh unto the Father, but
> by me. (John 14:16)

Deliverance is really a process that requires us to study the Bible under the guidance of the Holy Spirit and make the necessary changes in our lives to become more like Jesus. When we constantly follow the biblical laws and principles of the Bible, we are submitting to God, and demons and their works must flee from our lives (see James 4:7).

Again, knowledge is the most important aspect of our deliverance because the spirit of knowledge educates us and shows us what is right from what is wrong. It teaches us how to live the God-approved life. Spiritual knowledge and an understanding of God's Word defeat the spirit of ignorance, expose our real enemy, and show us how to fight and defeat him in the powerful name of Jesus.

The Bible, in 2 Timothy 2:15, tells us that we should study the Word of God to have God's approval in our lives. This studying of the Word goes deeper than just studying for an exam or other form of studying because when we study the Bible, we should allow the words from the printed pages of our Bibles to become a reality in our lives. In other words, we should do exactly what the Word says. It is just like baking a particular cake and following the recipe to get the exact result as stated by the designer or creator of that cake.

Doing exactly what the Word of God says helps us to become like the Word, who is Jesus the Christ. And when we are like Christ, we have the power over our enemies as stated in Luke 10:19. In addition, we have the powerful right to activate the law of Matthew 10.

> And when he had called unto him his twelve disciples, he gave them power against unclean spirits, to cast them out, and to heal all manner of sickness and all manner of disease. (Matthew 10:1)

Sharing God's Word

A very important aspect of maintaining our deliverance is to go and share the love of Christ with others. Becoming a disciple of Jesus. Teaching men and women boys and girls the divine principles of the Word that had changed our lives and set us free from the shackles (see also my other book, *Breaking Free from the Shackles of Witchcraft*). The law of Matthew 28:19-20 should become our mission as disciples of Jesus as stated below.

> Go ye therefore, and teach all nations, baptizing them in the name of the Father, and of the Son, and of the Holy Ghost: Teaching them to observe all things whatsoever I have commanded you: and, lo, I am with you always, even unto the end of the world. Amen. (Matthew 28:19–20)

When we dissect the powerful law of Mark 5:1–20, we observe the wicked and cruel works of demons in the life of a man, renamed the madman of Gadarenes. The demons of madness were taking total control of this man's life until the *Word*, who is Jesus the Christ, showed up. Deliverance shows up when Jesus shows up because it is the Word that brings about our deliverance. And when we are delivered, Jesus wants us to go and become testimonies of His goodness to others. So, He, Jesus, bids the delivered man to go and tell others of the good things that God had done in his life.

But the most important point I want us to see in the narrative below is how much of a distance Jesus would go to save just one soul. The loving and powerful ears of Jesus are open to our cries, and He will come all this way just to save you just like this demoniac in the narrative of Mark.

> And they came over unto the other side of the sea, into the country of the Gadarenes. And when he was come out of the ship, immediately there met him out of the tombs a man with an unclean spirit, Who had his dwelling among the tombs; and no man could bind him, no, not with chains: Because that he had been often bound with fetters and chains, and the chains had been plucked asunder by him, and the fetters broken in pieces: neither could any man tame him. And always, night and day, he was in the mountains, and in the tombs, crying, and cutting himself with stones. But when he saw Jesus afar off, he ran and worshipped him, And cried with a loud voice, and said, What have I to do with thee, Jesus, thou Son of the most high God? I adjure thee by God, that thou torment me not. For he said unto him, Come out of the man, thou unclean spirit. And he asked him, What is thy name? And he answered, saying, My name is Legion: for we are many. And he besought him much that he would not send them away out of the country. Now there was there nigh unto the mountains a great herd of swine feeding. And all the devils besought him, saying, Send us into the swine, that we may enter into them. And forthwith Jesus gave them leave. And the unclean spirits went out, and entered into the swine: and the

herd ran violently down a steep place into the sea, (they were about two thousand;) and were choked in the sea. And they that fed the swine fled, and told it in the city, and in the country. And they went out to see what it was that was done. And they come to Jesus, and see him that was possessed with the devil, and had the legion, sitting, and clothed, and in his right mind: and they were afraid. And they that saw it told them how it befell to him that was possessed with the devil, and also concerning the swine. And they began to pray him to depart out of their coasts. And when he was come into the ship, he that had been possessed with the devil prayed him that he might be with him. Howbeit Jesus suffered him not, but saith unto him, Go home to thy friends, and tell them how great things the Lord hath done for thee, and hath had compassion on thee. And he departed, and began to publish in Decapolis how great things Jesus had done for him: and all men did marvel. (Mark 5:1–20)

I must confess, like you, I had made all different types of promises to God, prior to the witchcraft attack that had almost taken away my life, only to be delivered out of a situation and find myself in a similar one because I did not follow through with my promise to God.

I did not maintain my deliverance. So, like the demonic man in Mark 5, I wanted to follow Jesus this time because I was delivered from demons and many of their activities that were killing, stealing, and destroying my life. I was ready to walk in the truth and the light this time.

God is amazing, and if you keep following Him in the way, He will no doubt use your mess and make it into beautiful messages for His great and powerful glory.

It is important for you to be aware that maintaining your deliverance takes deliberate effort, as you must choose every single day to live your life in God's ordained way. And not all people, including people in the building called churches, will be happy with your firm spiritual way of life. But you must choose God's way rather than man's way (see Jeremiah 17:5). It is a fact that every unconverted heart will hate the ways of the Lord as it is evil.

> For every one that doeth evil hateth the light, neither cometh to the light, lest his deeds should be reproved. (John 3:20)

Therefore, a great aspect of maintaining your deliverance is also for you to be aware that anywhere there are spiritual oppositions and battles, you should not run nor be afraid as these spiritual battles will make you stronger. The enemy will have to bow wherever and whenever the presence of God shows up. And if the Holy Spirit lives within you, power has shifted hand and the enemies will have to fall, just like Dagon, the Philistine's god.

Our God does not have to prove Himself or His power because He is the CEO of the universe and every power belongs to Him and all knees must bow.

Dagon, the god of the Philistine, did not only bow but he also crumbled in the presence of the Almighty God.

This great destruction of the enemy became a shock wave for the Philistines as it proved that there was a greater power in charge. And their idol is of no comparison to the power of our God.

So it will be with you if you continue to stand still in the face of opposition, at your place of work, school, home, the church, or wherever God places you; and trust God that the enemy will bow.

Do not be afraid of their faces, for God has made you this day a defenced city and an iron pillar and brazen walls against the whole land, against the kings of Judah, against the princes, the priests, and against the people of the land. Dagon must fall and crumble while the Ark of God marches on in victory as seen in the narrative of 1 Samuel 5.

> And the Philistines took the ark of God, and brought it from Ebenezer unto Ashdod. When the Philistines took the ark of God, they brought it into the house of Dagon, and set it by Dagon. And when they of Ashdod arose early on the morrow, behold, Dagon was fallen upon his face to the earth before the ark of the Lord. And they took Dagon, and set him in his place again. And when they arose early on the morrow morning, behold, Dagon was fallen upon his face to the ground before the ark of the Lord; and the head of Dagon and both the palms of his hands were cut off upon the threshold; only the stump of Dagon was left to him.
>
> Therefore neither the priests of Dagon, nor any that come into Dagon's house, tread on the threshold of Dagon in Ashdod unto this day. But the hand of the Lord was heavy upon them of Ashdod, and he destroyed them, and smote them with emerods, even Ashdod and the coasts thereof. (1 Samuel 5:1–6)

Another powerful way of maintaining your deliverance is to have the spiritual understanding that your body is the temple of God's Holy Spirit, and wherever you go, you are not alone as the Spirit of God goes with you as long as you are walking in obedience to divine authority.

And just like the Pharisees, the enemy in many who call themselves Christians will rise up against you because of your obedience to God. They will throw you out of the physical buildings called churches because you refuse to compromise your God-given principles. But like the blind man in the narrative of John, do not allow the devil to overpower your belief in God. Spiritual opposition always strengthens your faith in God if you are truly delivered. This blind man was delivered from the spirit of blindness—both physical and spiritual blindness. He was delivered from physical blindness when Jesus the Christ took mud and spit on it and made a mixture to put over his eyes; he washed his eye, and he was made to see. But his spiritual eyes began to open when the Pharisees disbanded him from their covens. He met Jesus the Christ and his spiritual eyes popped open. This will be the very same for you if you continue to walk in deliverance and refuse to compromise like this blind man in the gospel of John 9.

> And as Jesus passed by, he saw a man which was blind from his birth. And his disciples asked him, saying, Master, who did sin, this man, or his parents, that he was born blind? Jesus answered, Neither hath this man sinned, nor his parents: but that the works of God should be made manifest in him. I must work the works of him that sent me, while it is day: the night cometh, when no man can work. As long as I am in the world, I am the light of the world. When he had thus spoken, he spat on the ground, and made clay of the spittle, and he anointed the eyes of the blind man with the clay, And said unto him, Go, wash in the pool of Siloam, (which is by interpretation, Sent.) He went his way therefore, and washed, and came seeing.
>
> The neighbours therefore, and they which before had seen him that he was blind, said, Is not this he that sat and begged? Some said, This is he: others said, He is like him: but he said, I am he. Therefore said they unto him, How were thine eyes opened? He answered and said, A man that is called Jesus made clay, and anointed mine eyes, and said unto me, Go to the pool of Siloam, and wash: and I went and washed, and I received

sight. Then said they unto him, Where is he? He said, I know not. They brought to the Pharisees him that aforetime was blind. And it was the sabbath day when Jesus made the clay, and opened his eyes. Then again the Pharisees also asked him how he had received his sight. He said unto them, He put clay upon mine eyes, and I washed, and do see. Therefore said some of the Pharisees, This man is not of God, because he keepeth not the sabbath day. Others said, How can a man that is a sinner do such miracles? And there was a division among them. They say unto the blind man again, What sayest thou of him, that he hath opened thine eyes? He said, He is a prophet. But the Jews did not believe concerning him, that he had been blind, and received his sight, until they called the parents of him that had received his sight. And they asked them, saying, Is this your son, who ye say was born blind? how then doth he now see? His parents answered them and said, We know that this is our son, and that he was born blind: But by what means he now seeth, we know not; or who hath opened his eyes, we know not: he is of age; ask him: he shall speak for himself. These words spake his parents, because they feared the Jews: for the Jews had agreed already, that if any man did confess that he was Christ, he should be put out of the synagogue. Therefore said his parents, He is of age; ask him. Then again called they the man that was blind, and said unto him, Give God the praise: we know that this man is a sinner.

He answered and said, Whether he be a sinner or no, I know not: one thing I know, that, whereas I was blind, now I see. Then said they to him again, What did he to thee? how opened he thine eyes? He answered them, I have told you already, and ye did not hear: wherefore would ye hear it again? will ye also be his disciples? Then they reviled him, and said, Thou art his disciple; but we are Moses' disciples. We know that God spake unto Moses: as for this fellow, we know not from whence he is. The man answered and said unto them, Why herein is a marvellous thing, that ye know not from whence he is, and yet he hath opened mine eyes. Now we know that God heareth not sinners: but if any man be a worshipper of God, and doeth his will, him he heareth. Since the world began was it not heard that any man opened the eyes of one that was born blind. If this man were not of God, he could do nothing. They answered and said unto him, Thou wast altogether born in sins, and dost thou teach us? And they cast him out. Jesus heard that they had cast him out; and when he had found him, he said unto him, Dost thou believe on the Son of God? He answered and said, Who is he, Lord, that I might believe on him? And Jesus said unto him, Thou hast both seen him, and it is he that talketh with thee. And he said, Lord, I believe. And he worshipped him. (John 9:1–38)

In maintaining our deliverance, it is also important that we engage in deep spiritual warfare. You should become a habitual spiritual warrior, in the field of fasting and prayer.

As a matter of fact, spiritual fasting and prayer are mighty weapons that are used on the spiritual battlefield to disgrace the enemy. They are used to close the mouths of lions and to spiritually slay our Goliaths as we maintain our victorious deliverance in Jesus. Moreover, we must fast and pray to stop the demon(s) of our past from regaining entrance into our spirits and closing all doorways that will lead to any form of satanic oppression.

When we search through the Scriptures, our spiritual eyes will open to the power of a genuine fast. Daniel fasted for the nation of Israel and mighty things happened, see Daniel 10. We also witness Jehoshaphat fasted as the enemies gathered together and came up against him; power shifted hands because of his fast, and Jehoshaphat and his people claimed victory. See the full story in 2 Chronicles 20:3–30.

Esther fasted for the lives of the Jews, and a powerful spiritual exchange took place in the spirit realm. The physical manifestation was rewarding and the Jews were delivered from the enemies' hands. In addition, Haman, the enemy of the Jews, became the sacrifice on his own evil altar. See Esther 4: 16.

And most importantly, we witness Jesus the Christ setting this spiritual example of fasting and prayer for us as He fasted for forty days in the wilderness. See Matthew 4:1–11.

It is no exception for us; fasting gives supernatural power to the believers; and they who fast will find it easier to maintain their deliverance. No wonder Jesus reminded us in the law of Luke 5, that we must fast.

> But the days will come, when the bride-
> groom shall be taken away from them, and then
> shall they fast in those days. (Luke 5:35)

Finally, in maintaining our deliverance, we need to connect with other believers like ourselves. People who are walking in the truth according to the Word of God. The ones who seek to have spiritual oil in their lamps and are looking out through the eyes of faith for the bridegroom like the wise virgins in the narrative of Matthew 25 below.

> Then shall the kingdom of heaven be lik-
> ened unto ten virgins, which took their lamps,
> and went forth to meet the bridegroom. And five
> of them were wise, and five were foolish. They
> that were foolish took their lamps, and took no

oil with them: But the wise took oil in their vessels with their lamps. While the bridegroom tarried, they all slumbered and slept. And at midnight there was a cry made, Behold, the bridegroom cometh; go ye out to meet him. Then all those virgins arose, and trimmed their lamps. And the foolish said unto the wise, Give us of your oil; for our lamps are gone out. But the wise answered, saying, Not so; lest there be not enough for us and you: but go ye rather to them that sell, and buy for yourselves. And while they went to buy, the bridegroom came; and they that were ready went in with him to the marriage: and the door was shut. Afterward came also the other virgins, saying, Lord, Lord, open to us. But he answered and said, Verily I say unto you, I know you not. Watch therefore, for ye know neither the day nor the hour wherein the Son of man cometh.

As we continue to maintain our deliverance, let us remember that every day we should seek to improve our spiritual understanding of God's Word with the help of the Holy Spirit. The law of Revelation 1:7 should always be at the forefront of our minds as we drive out demons of doubts, fear, and the like out of our lives in Jesus the Christ: "Behold, he cometh with clouds; and every eye shall see him, and they also which pierced him: and all kindreds of the earth shall wail because of him. Even so, Amen" (Revelation 1:7). I bless you as you maintain your deliverance in Christ. Now go and tell others what He has done for you. Amen!

CHAPTER 9

101 Spiritual Warfare Prayers with Biblical Declarations to Overthrow the Evil Spirits of Sleeplessness and Infirmities in Jesus' name

Pray these prayers with unshakable faith and a strong belief in the power of God and His Word. Make sure that you repent of all known and unknown sins before engaging in this warfare section. Note, however, that a life of obedience to divine authority is the only life of victory, in Jesus the Christ.

> If you love me keep my commandments.
> (John 14:15)

1. By the blood of Jesus, I command every spirit of witchcraft to leave my life now, in the name of Jesus the Christ.
2. Evil altars that are speaking against my sleep, scatter by Holy Ghost fire, in the name of Jesus the Christ.
3. I sanction every spirit of jealousy to death, without mercy, by the power in the blood of Jesus the Christ.
4. Let every witchcraft curse return to its owner, in the name of Jesus the Christ.

5. By the blood of Jesus the Christ, I arrest every arrestor of my sleep, in the name of Jesus.

6. Lord, according to the law of Psalm 4:8, I must lay down and sleep when it's time for sleep. I therefore decree and declare by the power in the blood of Jesus that I shall sleep well this night and all the other nights to come, in the name of Jesus the Christ.

7. Let every anxious, tormenting spirit that has entered me be bound and cast out now, in the powerful name of Jesus the Christ.

8. I refuse to be oppressed by the spirit of sleeplessness, in the name of Jesus.

9. According to the law of Isaiah 49:26, I feed all my oppressors with their own flesh, and I give them their own blood to drink, in the name of Jesus the Christ.

10. I overcome the demon of sleeplessness by the blood of the lamb and the Word of my testimony, in the name of Jesus.

11. By the delivering blood of Jesus the Christ, I decree and declare that I am delivered from the demon of sleeplessness, in the name of Jesus the Christ.

12. I decree and declare this night that I shall sleep in peace, in the name of Jesus the Christ.

13. Blood of Jesus, I use You as a weapon of war against the evil spirit of sleeplessness, in the mighty name of Jesus the Christ.

14. By the blood of Jesus the Christ, I command all the enemies of my peace to scatter into confusion, in the name of Jesus.

15. Every effigy doll that represents me at any evil altar, burn to ashes and scatter into destruction, in the name of Jesus the Christ.

16. Devils, it is written, no weapon that is formed against me shall prosper, in the name of Jesus the Christ.

17. Spirit of hatred, you are an enemy to God and to me; therefore scatter, in the name of Jesus the Christ.

18. Thou Pharaoh of my sleep, be drowned in the Red Sea of confusion, in the powerful name of Jesus the Christ.

19. Any spirit of jealousy in my partner (husband or wife), I bind and cast you out, in the mighty name of Jesus.

20. Oh God, let my spirit reject the evil spirit of sleeplessness and torments, in the name of Jesus the Christ.

21. I decree and declare by the righteous blood of Jesus the Christ that, I will sleep for eight hours each night, in the name of Jesus the Christ.

22. In the name of Jesus the Christ, I decree and declare that I shall not take any sleeping medications; I shall close my eyes and go to sleep, in Jesus' name.

23. I bind and cast out every spirit of doubt, in the name of Jesus the Christ.

24. You, my bed, open up and receive the Holy Ghost fire, in the name of Jesus the Christ.

25. Let the great and terrible anger of the Lord chastise the enemy of sleeplessness in the name of Jesus the Christ.

26. I send the sword of the Lord into every evil coven and cauldron where my name and my sleep have been tied up, in the name of Jesus the Christ.

27. I stone the Goliath of my sleep, in the name of Jesus the Christ.

28. Every spirit of confusion that had entered my spirit because of the evil spirit of sleeplessness, I bind and cast you out, in the name of Jesus the Christ.

29. Spirit of tiredness, get out of me! In the name of Jesus the Christ.

30. I decree by the blood of Jesus the Christ that I shall live in the land of the living, in the name of Jesus the Christ.

31. Every spirit of heaviness in my head, I bind and cast you out, in the powerful name of Jesus the Christ.

32. I cancel all witchcraft dreams, and I break all evil covenants in the name of Jesus the Christ.

33. I decree and declare by the blood of Jesus that my enemies are dying in my stead, in the powerful name of Jesus the Christ.

34. I am prospering, and I am doing extremely well, in the name of Jesus the Christ.

35. I decree and declare by the blood of Jesus the Christ that my house is under the management of Jesus the Christ, in the name of Jesus.

36. I am a lover of God; the spirit of hatred is far from me, in the name of Jesus the Christ.

37. The spirit of forgiveness lives inside of me, and I forgive all those who hurt me, even before they ask, in the name of Jesus the Christ.

38. I am sleeping in safety because I am sleeping under the protective blood of Jesus the Christ, in the name of Jesus.

39. I have repented of all my sins, and now the authority and power to trample upon all the works of the enemies belong to me, in the name of Jesus the Christ.

40. I decree and declare by the power in the blood that God has turned my captivity captive, in the name of Jesus the Christ.

41. As I sing and praise my God, He had laid a spirit of ambushment for the enemy of sleeplessness, in the name of Jesus the Christ.

42. For the enemy of sleeplessness, I see today, I shall see him no more, in the name of Jesus the Christ.

43. According to the law of Psalm 1:3, I decree and declare by the wonderful blood of Jesus Christ that this day, I am flourishing like a tree that is planted by the rivers of water, in the name of Jesus the Christ.

44. I decree and declare by the undefeated blood of Jesus Christ that all my Hamans are hanged by their own wickedness, in the name of Jesus Christ.

45. I decree and declare by the blood of Jesus Christ that I am in love with Jesus, and I am walking daily, in obedience, to all His commandments, in the name of Jesus Christ.

46. I decree and declare that the blood of Jesus Christ closes all the lions' mouths, in the name of Jesus.

47. I decree and declare by the speaking blood of Jesus Christ that all my steps are ordered by the Lord, in the name of Jesus.

48. I decree and declare by the healing blood of Jesus the Christ, all demons and their activities have left my body, in the overcoming name of Jesus the Christ.

49. I decree and declare by the healing blood of Jesus the Christ that every day, I am mounting up like an eagle, and my strength is renewed in God, in the name of Jesus the Christ.

50. I decree and declare by the healing blood of Jesus the Christ that I am called by the name of the Lord; therefore, I am healed this day and wickedness is far from me, in the name of Jesus.

51. Let the evil foundation of my father's and mother's houses scatter into shame, in the name of Jesus the Christ.

52. Let every ancestral altar of wickedness scatter into madness in the name of Jesus the Christ.

53. Every demonic programming of my sleep in the heavenly, I pull you down with the blood of Jesus, in the name of Jesus the Christ.

54. God, in the name of Jesus, let the plans of the enemy backfire, in the name of Jesus Christ.

55. For Jesus the Christ has disarmed principalities and powers, so let the powerful finger of God arise and write the judgment of the wicked witches that are working against me and my family, in the name of Jesus Christ.

56. Life and death are in the power of the tongue; therefore, I use my tongue and speak death to the spirits of restlessness and sleeplessness, in the mighty name of Jesus.

57. I command every stronghold of sleeplessness, restlessness, and torment to collapse and die in the victorious name of Jesus.

58. I am more than a conqueror, in the name of Jesus the Christ.

59. And God shall keep me in perfect peace because my mind is stayed on Him; therefore, let all enemies of my peace be restless, in the name of Jesus the Christ.

60. I scatter all evil altars and break all their curses and covenants working against my sleep, in the name of Jesus.

61. I decree by the thunder of God's power that the enemy of sleeplessness is destroyed, in the powerful name of Jesus Christ.

62. I break all witchcraft shackles off my life and that of my sleep, in the powerful blood of Jesus Christ.

63. Let the cleansing blood of Jesus Christ wash away every evil mark of the water spirit from my sleep, in the mighty name of Jesus Christ.

64. I command every unbroken curse to be broken now, by the blood of Jesus Christ.

65. I command every evil river flowing into my sleep to dry up, in the powerful name of Jesus Christ.

66. Stubborn enemies of my sleep, die, in the name of Jesus Christ.

67. Ancestral spirits crying against my sleep be silent, by the speaking blood of Jesus Christ, in the name of Jesus.

68. I decree and declare by the speaking blood of Jesus the Christ that on the first day of my fast, all the enemies will be engulfed by the spirit of trembling, in the name of Jesus.

69. I decree and declare that I have great peace because I love the laws of the Lord, in the name of Jesus.

70. I decree and declare that I am always dressed in the armor of the Lord, and I am ready for battle, in the victorious name of Jesus the Christ.

71. I decree and declare that my heart is merry, and my health is excellent, in the name of Jesus the Christ.

72. I decree and declare by the protecting blood of Jesus the Christ that every day, I have been preserved by the powerful hands of almighty God, in the name of Jesus.

73. I decree and declare by the speaking blood of Jesus the Christ that the Lord Himself is my rock and my fortress, my deliverer and my strength, my buckler and the horn of my salvation, in the mighty name of Jesus.

74. I decree and declare by the blood of Jesus Christ that the enemies of my sleep have been smitten by the bow of steel from God's army, in the name of Jesus.

75. Every Judas of my sleep, run mad, in the powerful name of Jesus the Christ.

76. Every evil eye looking into my destiny, be blinded now, in the powerful name of Jesus the Christ.

77. The evil weapon used against my sleep, dry up, by the power in the name of Jesus the Christ.

78. Gossiping tongue that speaks against my rest, be silenced by the speaking blood of Jesus the Christ.

79. Lord, let all the evil hands that are lifted against my life be paralyzed, in the name of Jesus the Christ.

80. I challenge all my oppressors, by the power in the blood and the name of Jesus the Christ.

81. Weapon of destruction lifted against my sleep, go back to your sender now, in the name of Jesus the Christ.

82. Lord, whenever and wherever my name and that of my family members are called for evil, answer the calls, in the great and powerful name of Jesus the Christ.

83. I decree and declare this day that the Word of the Lord is established in my life, home, and family, in the name of Jesus the Christ.

84. Satan nor his agents do not have the legal rights to my destiny, in the name of Jesus the Christ.

85. Let the rain of the Lord saturate my life today, in the name of Jesus the Christ.

86. I am a servant of the Lord, and I am healed in His great name.

87. As of today, whatever I put my hands to do, shall prosper, in the name of Jesus the Christ.

88. Like Elijah, I call down the fire of the Lord to consume the hands of the wicked against my life and family, in the name of Jesus the Christ.

89. I decree and declare that the Lord is God, and He is on my side, in the name of Jesus the Christ.

90. Lord, in the name of Jesus the Christ, let my life glorify you, in Jesus' name.

91. Blessed be the Lord, for He has shown me His marvelous kindness in the restoration of my sleep and my life in the name of Jesus the Christ.

92. I decree and declare that devils cannot curse that which God has blessed, and I am healed in Jesus' name.

93. I command Balaam's twenty-one evil altars to attack him, in the name of Jesus the Christ.

94. Let all my enemies be silent; the Lord my God is calling my name for great success, in the name of Jesus the Christ.

95. I decree and declare by the powerful blood of Jesus the Christ that evil altars set up against me and my family have been rented, and the ashes of destruction are now pouring out on their heads and that of their children, in the name of Jesus the Christ.

96. I decree and declare by the blood of Jesus the Christ that the horns of the wicked against my sleep have been cut off this day, in the mighty name of Jesus the Christ.

97. My flesh and my heart failed, but God is the strength of my heart, and my portion forever, in the name of Jesus the Christ.

98. Unto Thee, O Lord, do I give thanks, in the name of Jesus the Christ.

99. I decree and declare now that at midnight, I will arise and praise thy name, in the name of Jesus the Christ.

100. I am blessed and highly favored; I am a child of the King, in the name of Jesus the Christ.

101. I command every spiritual enemy to leave my bed now, in the name of Jesus the Christ.

102. I sprinkle the protective blood of Jesus the Christ on my pillow, and I shall sleep, in the name of Jesus.

103. Every terror of the nights that has been programmed against my sleep, receive the Holy Ghost fire, and return to your sender, in the name of Jesus the Christ.

104. You, the ancestral spirit of my sleep, I bind and cast you out, in the name of Jesus the Christ.

105. Triangular powers of the nights, be disturbed, by the blood of Jesus the Christ.

106. Every enchantment and divination that is set against my sleep, catch your owner, in the name of Jesus the Christ.

107. The demonic iron pen that is writing my name for evil, burn to ashes and scatter, in the mighty name of Jesus the Christ.

108. Spirit of manipulation that is working against my sleep, backfire, by the blood of Jesus, in the name of Jesus the Christ.

109. I command every blood sacrifice that is crying against my sleep from any graveyard to be silenced, by the powerful blood of Jesus the Christ.

110. Spiritual serpents and scorpions tormenting my sleep, I trample upon you in the name of Jesus the Christ.

111. Now that I am healed and delivered, I shall maintain my deliverance, in the name of Jesus the Christ. Amen!

PERSONAL NOTES

_____
_____
_____
_____
_____
_____
_____
_____
_____
_____
_____
_____
_____
_____
_____
_____
_____
_____

My Personal Goal as It Relates to Maintaining My Deliverance

_____
_____
_____
_____
_____
_____

The end!

ABOUT THE AUTHOR

Sweda has been under severe demonic witchcraft attacks. But spiritual ignorance was the fuel that the enemy weaponized and used to almost destroy her life. The spirit of sleeplessness almost claimed her life, but the power of God's Word became that powerful spiritual weapon that was used against this wicked principality. The Bible is clear; it is through knowledge and its application that the author (the captive) was set free (Proverbs 11:9b).

Therefore, the author now listens to the powerful voice of God, in writing books about the biblical principles that she had used to become totally free from the spirits of anxiety, restlessness, sleeplessness, and all the demonic oppressions that came from evil altars, in the victorious name of Jesus the Christ.

It was and still is Sweda's personal pledge made to God that if He freed her from the powers of witchcraft, which was strangulating her sleep, her health, her family, and her finances, she would thereby use her experience and deliverance as testimonies of encouragement to help others who are held down by these demonic forces to be freed also.

Sweda has been freed from the evil spirit of sleeplessness, and she now lives a very healthy, happy life in Jesus. Sweda is a teacher by profession and has studied at the graduate level. She was born in Jamaica. She also writes devotionals and lives with her family and their dog, Chase. She loves the Lord with all her heart, and she desires that all who are bound by this evil spirit of sleeplessness, be free, in the powerful name of Jesus the Christ.

Printed in the USA
CPSIA information can be obtained
at www.ICGtesting.com
LVHW020047060324
773596LV00001B/59